This Catalogue is presented as a
benefit of your membership. The exhibitions
and programs of the Los Angeles County
Museum of Art would not have been
possible without your support.

D0054375

Thames & Hudson world of art

This famous series provides the widest available
range of illustrated books on art in all its aspects.

If you would like to receive a complete list
of titles in print please write to:

THAMES & HUDSON
181A High Holborn
London WC1V 7QX

In the United States please write to:

THAMES & HUDSON INC.
500 Fifth Avenue
New York, New York 10110

Printed in Singapore

LOS ANGELES COUNTY MUSEUM OF ART

WITH 197 ILLUSTRATIONS, 184 IN COLOR

LOS ANGELES COUNTY MUSEUM OF ART

For the Los Angeles County Museum of Art
Director of Publications: Stephanie Emerson
Project Manager: Nola Butler
Editors: Matt Stevens and Nola Butler
Designer: Catherine Lorenz
Photography Supervisor: Peter Brenner
Rights and Reproductions: Cheryle T. Robertson, with Shaula Coyl

Note to the reader
Not every work of art included in this book will be on view at all times.

The first group of digits in the acquisition numbers (found at the end of the captions for illustrated objects) indicates the year the work was acquired by the museum.

Key to abbreviations used in this book
cb.   center back
diam.   diameter
h.   height

First published in paperback in the United States of America in 2003 by Thames & Hudson Inc., 500 Fifth Avenue, New York, New York 10110

thamesandhudsonusa.com

Library of Congress Catalog Card Number 2002111486
ISBN 0-500-20360-1

Printed and bound in Singapore by CS Graphics

Cover and details
Georges de La Tour, *The Magdalen with the Smoking Flame* (p. 97); p. 2: *Archangel Raphael* (p. 113); p. 3: Pablo Picasso, *Weeping Woman with Handkerchief* (p. 211); p. 4: *Quail amid Autumn Grasses and Flowers* (p. 70); p. 5: Michiel Sweerts, *Plague in an Ancient City* (p. 99); p. 6: Benedetto Luti, *Head of an Apostle* (p. 106); p. 7: *Shiva as Lord of the Dance* (p. 38); p. 8: David Hockney, *Mulholland Drive: The Road to the Studio* (p. 224); p. 11: *Ardabil Carpet* (p. 58); p. 12: Edgar Degas, *Giovanna and Giuliana Bellelli* (p. 120); p. 14: Vincent van Gogh, *The Postman Joseph Roulin* (p. 126); p. 17: *Jar with Peony Sprays and Lotuses* (p. 53); p. 18: *Round-Topped Stela of Iuf-er-bak* (p. 84); p. 228: Imogen Cunningham, *Aloe Bud* (p. 188)

CONTENTS

FOREWORD

In the fifteen years since the Los Angeles County Museum of Art (LACMA) published its preceding handbook, the institution has changed physically and programmatically in remarkable ways. Like any art museum, however, the permanent collection remains its defining feature. This completely revised handbook includes important new acquisitions as well as many of our familiar landmark works of art.

The brief texts were written by LACMA's curatorial staff, the experts charged with the acquisition, research, and exhibition of the collections. (Contributors are cited on p. 19.) Both the selection of objects and the interpretive commentaries demonstrate the significance of these individual works of art within the permanent collection. In addition to introducing recently acquired works, the handbook provides a forum for the presentation of new scholarship, including the latest attributions and datings.

The five sections of the book—Asian Art, European Art, Latin American Art, American Art, and Modern and Contemporary Art—reflect LACMA's collaborative curatorial organization. This interdisciplinary approach, also evident in the museum's installations, is designed to make the interpretation of our collections more accessible, coherent, and revealing. With these goals in mind, the curators have opted for different strategies within each section of the handbook, sometimes arranging works chronologically, as in the European Art section, at other times assembling the objects thematically, as in the section devoted to Asian art. The result is neither a comprehensive catalogue of the permanent collection nor a definitive statement about its organization. Rather, this representative selection is meant to enhance the visitor's experience as well as attract a new audience to the museum.

Some of the works in the handbook came to LACMA as individual acquisitions; others were obtained through gifts or purchases of extensive collections. From its inception as part of the Los Angeles Museum of History, Science and Art at the original site in Exposition Park in 1910, through its founding as a separate institution at its present location in Hancock Park in 1965, the museum has relied on the generous gifts of many donors to develop its permanent collection. A number of these individuals and foundations are credited in the entries for the illustrated objects. Because this publication is representative, rather than all-inclusive, numerous highly valued gifts and purchased works of art unfortunately do not appear in these pages.

We anticipate that LACMA's collection will continue to grow as we strive to present it in meaningful ways. Most recently, it has been enhanced by three major acquisitions—the Moore Collection of Korean Art, the Bernard and Edith Lewin Collection of Mexican Art, and the Madina Collection of Islamic Art. I hope that you will share my great pleasure in witnessing the expanding scope of LACMA's permanent collection and, in turn, its reflection of the diverse local and international community that serves as our museum-going audience.

Andrea L. Rich
President and Director

CONTRIBUTORS

Austen B. Bailly

Stephanie Barron

Sheri Bernstein

Robert L. Brown

Martin Chapman

Carol S. Eliel

Virginia Fields

Ilene Susan Fort

Howard N. Fox

Dale Carolyn Gluckman

Hollis Goodall

Sharon Goodman

Burglind Jungmann

Wendy Kaplan

Ilona Katzew

Melinda Klayman

Linda Komaroff

Jo Lauria

Mary L. Levkoff

June Li

J. Patrice Marandel

Stephen Markel

Bruce Robertson

Sandra L. Rosenbaum

Kevin Salatino

Robert T. Singer

Robert A. Sobieszek

Kaye Durland Spilker

Sharon Sadako Takeda

Nancy Thomas

Saleema Waraich

J. Keith Wilson

Lynn Zelevansky

ASIAN ART

Vessel

Japan, Niigata or Nagano prefecture, middle Jōmon period,
c. 3000–2000 B.C.
Coil-built earthenware with incised, modeled, and applied decoration
H. 22 1/8 in. (56.2 cm)
William T. Sesnon Jr. Bequest
M.81.62.1

THIS IMPRESSIVE STONE AGE VESSEL reflects the remarkable character of Japan's earliest ceramic culture. The massive container was decorated with incised patterns enhanced by applied leather-hard strings of clay. The exuberant surface design is organized in four registers divided by raised bands. The sunken waist, marked by projecting lugs, separates the tall vertical spirals at the bottom from the horizontal waves and small open loops on the swelling shoulder above. The mouth is enriched with animated open crests that reach into space. After it was decorated, the jar was baked on an open bonfire.

Magnificently expressive "flame-style" pots were made during the middle Jōmon period in the inland, forested areas of Niigata prefecture, near the Japan Sea, and in neighboring Nagano prefecture. Now called the "Snow Country," the region had warmer weather in ancient times. An abundance of food and supplies provided social stability to hunter-gatherer societies, allowing them to create large, ornately decorated vessels. Although the ceramics appear nonfunctional, they were in fact used for cooking, perhaps of a ritual nature.

Seated Female Figure

Northern Afghanistan, Namazga V–VI,
c. 2500–1500 B.C.

Chlorite and limestone

H. 5 1/4 in. (13.3 cm)

Purchased with funds provided by Phil Berg

M.2000.1a–f

THE BRONZE AGE CULTURE of Bactria (3000–1500 B.C.), located in present-day Afghanistan, defines the easternmost edge of a broad band of ancient trade routes from Iran to Central Asia. The museum's collection of Bactrian art is one of the most significant in the United States and includes bronze compartmented seals, lead ceremonial objects, chlorite vessels, jewelry, small columns of variegated stone, as well as this seated female figure.

Figural sculpture from Central Asia is exceedingly rare. The restricted corpus includes a number of examples of a seated female constructed from a variety of different types of stone. The figures, dressed in heavy enveloping cloaks, have simplified facial features with large blank eyes. The garment is usually incised with a pattern of twisted strands, probably indicating a woolen model. On this example, the figure's hair is rendered in black chlorite, showing a complex arrangement that encircles the head. The characteristic face, though somewhat eroded, is expressive. The chalky arms are also worn and provide no indication of their original position. The placement of a rarely preserved element—a single foot—is suggested by the channel at the right hem of the garment.

The heavy robe provides a link to imagery from Iran. A silver vessel of the late third millennium B.C., believed to be from the area near Persepolis, shows a similar seated woman. Later Iranian cylinder seals, found at Tell-i Malyan and Susa, evidence the continued appeal of the subject into the second millennium B.C.

Ritual Wine Storage Jar

China, late Shang dynasty, early Anyang phase, c. 1300–1200 B.C.

Cast bronze

H. 13 3/4 in. (34.9 cm)

Gift of Mr. and Mrs. Eric Lidow

AC1998.251.1

IN ANCIENT CHINA, BRONZE WAS EMPLOYED to create efficient weapons and tools. It was also used to cast special wine and food containers reserved to honor deceased family members in elaborate ritual banquets. This heavy wine bucket (*zun* in Chinese) reflects the remarkable style, extraordinary technical accomplishment, and material wealth associated with the Shang dynasty (c. 1500–1050 B.C.).

The original owner of the uninscribed ritual container was a person of high standing, perhaps rewarded with the privilege of possessing such an important object through service to the Shang king. The vessel was later buried in a tomb either because it was viewed as an essential element for the

continuation of ancestor worship even after death or because it was seen as a treasured possession. Preserved underground for millennia, it was probably excavated by chance in the early twentieth century.

Ashurnasirpal II and a Winged Deity

Iraq, Nimrud, Neo-Assyrian period, c. 870 B.C.

Gypseous alabaster

90 3/4 x 83 in. (230.5 x 210.8 cm)

Purchased with funds provided by Anna Bing Arnold

66.4.3

THE MOST MONUMENTAL AND IMPRESSIVE objects from the museum's ancient West Asian collection are five massive stone panels from the Northwest Palace of Ashurnasirpal II, the king of ancient Assyria from 883 to 858 B.C. Several palaces were located at the site, on high ground near the juncture of the Zab and Tigris Rivers. Strategically situated, the royal capital and military center overlooked rich plains in what is now central Iraq.

The interior walls of the royal apartments and public rooms, such as audience halls and administrative areas, were lined with stone reliefs, often depicting the king performing ritual ceremonies accompanied by divine beings. This panel was probably originally located in Room H of the king's private apartment. On it, a winged deity follows the king and raises one hand in a gesture of benediction or divine protection. Ashurnasirpal II carries a bow and a shallow libation vessel. The figures wear heavy fringed tunics with decorative bands of floral or geometric motifs along the hems. Each figure carries two knives, tucked into the waistband of the garments, and wears an elaborate assemblage of armbands, earrings, beads, and bracelets.

The reliefs are characterized by a detailed and highly linear treatment of all elements. Lines of cuneiform text run across this and other examples and are known as the "standard inscription" of Ashurnasirpal II because they were repeated, with slight variations, on each panel throughout the palace. The repetitive text proclaims the king's legitimacy, authority, and accomplishments.

Tomb Sculpture of a Chimera

China, probably Sichuan Province, Eastern Han dynasty, 25–220

Molded earthenware with traces of applied decoration and paint

$16^5/_8$ x $15^5/_8$ x $10^1/_2$ in. (42.8 x 39.7 x 26.7 cm)

Gift of Elly Nordskog and family in memory of Bob Nordskog

AC1997.1.1

IN GRAVES NEAR THE END of the Bronze Age in China, *mingqi*, or "spirit objects" (painted or glazed earthenwares specifically made for the dead), began to replace more valuable cast bronzes, carved jades, and lacquers. By Han times (206 B.C.– A.D. 220), ceramic vessels and figural sculpture dominated the contents of Chinese burials.

The museum's chimera combines a crouching feline body with a long neck and snarling muzzle, winglike tufts, and a horn on either side of a pronounced bump at the crown of the head. Not an everyday creature, this is a fantastic composite influenced by imaginary visualizations first developed by China's neighbors to the west. It corresponds to a mythical beast called a *bixie* (which literally means "to avoid evil"), first described in Chinese texts datable to the second century B.C.

Such earthenware figures, typically created in pairs, were placed in tombs to protect against malevolent spirits. The animation of the pose recalls a range of burial pieces created in the southwestern province of Sichuan. Related guardian figures were also executed in a larger scale in stone, standing above ground to mark important tombs in Sichuan and the lower Yangzi River valley in southeastern China.

Tomb Sculpture of a Seated Warrior

Japan, late Tumulus period, c. 500–600

Coil-built earthenware with applied decoration

31 x 14⅜ x 15 in. (78.7 x 36.5 x 38.1 cm)

Mr. and Mrs. Allan C. Balch Fund

M.58.9.4

THIS BEGUILING FIGURE OF A SEATED WARRIOR was used to decorate the tomb of a noble during the Tumulus period (250–600). Originating in the mid-second century as simple cylindrical forms, *haniwa* evolved into more complex figural representations of houses, weapons, animals, and humans. Regardless of subject, they were placed either low along the bank of a keyhole-shaped tomb mound, opposite the entrance, or clustered near the tomb door. *Haniwa* had to be constructed quickly upon the death of a noble

in preparation for burial. The resulting simplicity of their design imbues them with a mysterious quietness.

The museum's warrior, identified by his helmet and sword, wears a belted tunic, trousers, and beads. His hands, positioned in front of his chest, probably held a spear. The reddish low-fired clay is typical, as are the neatly cut eye and mouth holes.

Pensive Bodhisattva

Pakistan, Gandhara region, Kushan period, c. 200–300

Gray schist

22 x 11 x 6 $\frac{1}{4}$ in. (55.9 x 27.9 x 15.9 cm)

Gift of Henry and Ruth Trubner in honor of the museum's twenty-fifth anniversary and to honor
Dr. Pratapaditya Pal

AC1994.8.1

THE ANCIENT COSMOPOLITAN REGION known as Gandhara lay at the confluence of the lucrative international trade routes between Rome, India, and China, in what is now Pakistan and bordering Afghanistan. From the first to the third century, the mighty Kushan dynasty ruled from Gandhara in the north to the heartland of India in the south. Buddhist sculpture, particularly images of the Buddha and bodhisattvas, were prevalent at the time.

Bodhisattvas are potential Buddhas who choose to remain on earth to help living beings in their quest for enlightenment. Unlike the Buddha, typically shown dressed as a monk, bodhisattvas wear the clothing of lay princes, including a turban and elaborate jewelry. The strongly modeled chest, heavy garments, and carefully delineated drapery folds of the museum's bodhisattva characterize Greco-Roman artistic traditions. The meaningful pose of the figure also derives from Western models introduced through trade between Gandhara and the Roman world. The deity sits on a stool, his right leg crossed over his left, and raises one finger to his face. With a slightly cocked head and narrowed eyes, the composition recalls the quintessential Western posture of contemplation. Over time, it came to represent meditation in a variety of Buddhist contexts and was particularly popular in China, Korea, and Japan.

The Aristocratic Women

Pakistan, Gandhara region, Kushan period, c. 100–200

Gray schist

23 1/8 x 13 3/4 x 6 in. (58.7 x 34.9 x 15.2 cm)

Purchased with funds provided by Mrs. Harry Lenart, Robert and Mary Looker, Robert F. Maguire III, and The Hillcrest Foundation through the 1998 Collectors Committee, Stephen Markel in memory of Catherine W. Markel, the Southern Asian Art Council, and S. Sanford and Charlene S. Kornblum

AC1999.3.1

AS EXQUISITE AS IT IS RARE, this sensitive double portrait epitomizes the syncretic art of Gandhara at its finest. The naturalistic figures are elegantly garbed in fashions popular among the aristocracy of second-century Rome. The subject, however, is most likely a parable about two unnamed women in an incident from one of the past lives of the founder of Buddhism, Buddha Shakyamuni (traditionally dated c. 563–483 B.C.).

According to the legend recounted in the *Maha-Ummagga Jataka* (The Story of the great tunnel), the future Buddha overheard two women quarreling over a scented necklace made of brightly colored entwined threads. He asked each of the women to name the perfume she had placed on the necklace. The Buddha-to-be then dropped the necklace into a bowl of hot water and asked a perfume merchant to identify the scent. He did so, and the legitimate owner was revealed.

Buddha Shakyamuni

India, probably Uttar Pradesh, Gupta period, c. 550–600

Cast brass with pigment

15 1/2 x 6 3/4 x 4 in. (39.4 x 17.1 x 10.2 cm)

Gift of the Michael J. Connell Foundation

M.70.17

THE GUPTA PERIOD (320–600) is celebrated as a high point in the art and culture of India, the moment when Buddhist, Hindu, and Jain sculpture achieved a balance between otherworldly idealism and human sensuality. The combined reflection of the spiritual and corporeal is a chief characteristic of this alluring Buddha image. The deity's robe clings to the body, revealing wide shoulders and a gentle sway of the hips. As with all Buddha images, the display of the hands has symbolic importance. Here, the Buddha raises his right hand to reveal the palm, inviting worshipers to approach without fear. The lowered eyes likewise suggest gentleness and accessibility.

This refined sculpture was made in northern India in the late sixth century. It was later taken to Tibet where blue pigment was daubed over the hair curls in accordance with Tibetan practice. Its transfer to a Tibetan monastery saved it from suffering the fate of so many other northern Indian Buddhist copper alloy sculptures, which were melted down over the centuries for their content.

Jizō

Japan, late Heian period, c. 1070–1120

Wood

75 1/8 (including base) x 24 x 24 in. (190.8 x 61 x 61 cm)

Gift of Anna Bing Arnold

M.74.117

THIS MONUMENTAL IMAGE possesses many attributes of a Buddhist monk. His head is shaven, thus lacking the small curls of the Buddha's closely cropped hair. His empty right hand is positioned to grasp a *shakujō* (jingle staff), one of a monk's eighteen possessions, which he tapped on the ground to warn insects and small animals of his approaching footsteps.

This is not simply a monk, however, but a bodhisattva named Jizō who became extremely popular among Japanese Buddhists following the introduction of Buddhism to Japan in the sixth century. Jizō was especially important among "Pure Land" sect believers, who looked forward to rebirth in Buddhist paradise. He was worshiped as the protector of children, mothers in childbirth, travelers, and others in distress.

Like many Buddhist deities, the museum's Jizō stands on a lotus base. The pure flower rises above murky waters, symbolizing release from the karmic wheel of rebirth. In his left hand, Jizō holds a wish-granting jewel attesting to his transcendent power. The enlightened character of the deity is also manifested by the elongated ears and third eye, indicated by an inset jewel in the center of the forehead. The large head, broad brow, and small, delicate features convey the gentle benevolence and approachability found in the finest bodhisattva images of the late Heian period.

Buddha Amitayus

Tibet, probably Phanyul Valley, about 1170–1189

Thangka; opaque watercolor and gold on linen

102 x 69 in. (259.1 x 175.3 cm)

From the Nasli and Alice Heeramaneck Collection, Museum Associates Purchase

M.84.32.5

AMONG THE MOST DISTINCTIVE and revered forms of Asian art are Tibetan *thangka* paintings. Rolled for storage and transport, *thangka*s are rectangular images painted with ground mineral pigments on cotton or linen. Most were originally graced with narrow silk borders, plain or brocade silk mounts, and gossamer silk covers that were gathered at the top to serve as decorative swags when the paintings were displayed over an altar.

This exceptionally large, early *thangka* features Amitayus, the cosmic Buddha of endless life. The deity sits on a lotus pedestal holding a vase containing the elixir of immortality. He is flanked on the viewer's left by Avalokiteshvara, the bodhisattva of compassion; on the right is Maitreya, the bodhisattva of wisdom. Monks and additional bodhisattvas pay homage above while three more bodhisattvas appear below. Hayagriva (in the lower left) and Achala (in the lower right) are fierce protectors of the faith.

A dedicatory inscription unobtrusively placed among the lotus petals under Amitayus records that the painting was made to honor Choki Gyeltsen (1121–1189), an important Buddhist monk of the Kadampa order who apparently resided in one of the monasteries in the Phanyul Valley northeast of Lhasa. The inscription reads, "This picture, made by Chogyen, marks the life-attainment ceremony of the Lama Choki Gyeltsen at Cangragnaga in Bayul. Good Fortune!"

Votive Panel with Jambhala

China, early Ming period, c. 1400–1425

Silk and metal-thread embroidery on plain-weave silk

15 $5/8$ x 7 $1/4$ in. (39.7 x 18.4 cm)

Costume Council Fund

M.88.121

JAMBHALA, THE GOD OF WEALTH, serves as a powerful protector of the Buddhist faith. In this elegant embroidery, he holds in one hand a noose for subduing enemies and in the other a jewel-spitting mongoose with the power to vanquish serpents. The deity is seated on a lotus throne, sheltered by a *prabha torana* (arch of light) formed of tricolor clouds that emanate from baskets also containing lotuses in bloom. In the lower section, scrolling vines

and additional lotus flowers sprout from a rendering of the Sacred Peaks; each blossom supports a Sanskrit character in Tibetan Lantsa script worked in gold thread. The characters represent the syllables of a mantra, a formula of words and sounds that possesses magical or divine power.

This votive panel is one of a dozen known examples featuring Buddhas, bodhisattvas, and guardian figures that are remarkably consistent in design and technique. Based on their style and quality, the embroideries are thought to have been made in China during the early Ming dynasty to serve as imperial gifts to important Tibetan Buddhist temples. Relations between China's rulers and the lamas who led the major Buddhist orders were extremely strong during the reign of Yongle (1402–24), the third Ming emperor.

Tŏksewi, 153rd of the 500 Nahan

Korea, middle Chosŏn dynasty, dated 1562

Hanging scroll; ink and color on silk

$50^3/_4$ x $15^1/_2$ in. (128.9 x 39.4 cm)

Murray Smith Fund

M.84.112

BUDDHISM REACHED KOREA via China in the mid-fourth century and prospered under royal patronage until the end of the Koryŏ dynasty (918–1392). The establishment of the Chosŏn dynasty in 1392 challenged the power, popularity, and character of Korean Buddhism. Taejo (reigned 1392–98), first king of the ruling house, founded his regime on neo-Confucian tenets borrowed from China. Despite the ascendancy of the new doctrine, Buddhism continued to flourish among certain segments of the population.

This beautiful image depicts a haloed figure studying a sutra scroll inscribed with religious teachings. The scroll also bears an inscription that identifies the subject as Tŏksewi, one of the 500 *nahan*, or disciples, of the Buddha Shakyamuni. The painting was one of 200 scrolls commissioned by the Dowager Queen Munjŏng (1501–1565) to ensure the long life of her son King Myŏngjong (reigned 1545–67) and the well-being and success of all her descendants. This is the only painting from the group known to survive.

Sŏn (Chinese: Chan; Japanese: Zen) Buddhists believed that enlightenment could be reached through personal efforts. Thus, images of mystical deities were much less inspiring than those featuring human subjects such as disciples, patriarchs, and teachers. This informal depiction, showing the figure in a three-quarter view seated in a natural outdoor setting, conforms to compositions of a more secular character.

Shiva as Lord of the Dance

India, Tamil Nadu, Chola period, c. 950–1000

Cast copper alloy

30 x 22 1/2 x 7 in. (76.2 x 57.2 x 17.8 cm)

Anonymous gift

M.75.1

THIS PROCESSIONAL IMAGE represents the Hindu god Shiva as Lord of
the Dance surrounded by a ring of fire. In Hinduism, Shiva is worshiped as
the destroyer and restorer in a theological triad with the gods Vishnu and
Brahma, who represent preservation and creation. This form of the deity
became popular in the early tenth century during the Chola period

(850–1278) in southern India. According to the traditional interpretation, Shiva, spinning on one foot and trampling a midget representing ignorance, personifies the axis of the world, his dance setting the universe into action.

As is true of certain Buddhist images showing Tantric deities, the supernatural powers of Hindu gods are depicted with a multiplicity of arms. In this sculpture, the upper pair of arms holds symbols of creation and destruction—a drum and flame—while the gracefully posed lower pair suggests reassurance and victory over ignorance. Combined, these gestures signify Shiva's grace as he guides believers to the path of liberation. Shiva's compassion is underscored by the small image personifying the river goddess Ganga (Ganges) in the fanned strands of his hair. Shiva used his hair to save humankind by breaking the celestial river's fall to earth.

Jagadeva (India, Gujarat, active c. 1130–70)

Sarasvati, dated 1153

Marble

47 1/4 x 19 3/4 x 11 3/4 in. (120 x 50.2 x 29.8 cm)

Gift of Anna Bing Arnold

M.86.83

JAINISM, THE THIRD MAJOR RELIGION of India, has been practiced continuously since the sixth century B.C., if not earlier. Like Buddhism, it evolved as a popular reaction against the caste-bound and ritual-oriented Hinduism. Jainism shares with Buddhism and Hinduism several deities, such as Sarasvati, the goddess of learning, knowledge, and music.

Carved in white marble, this image of Sarasvati is the embodiment of the medieval Indian concept of ideal feminine beauty. Elegantly poised, her voluptuous body is rendered with a heightened sense of fluidity and sensuality. In each of her two upper arms she holds a lotus stem encircling a pair of geese, a symbol of purity. Her broken lower right arm would have displayed the gesture of charity or carried an ascetic's water flask, while her lower left hand once held a book. Two small flanking musicians allude to her role as the prime teacher of music while larger female attendants hold honorific flywhisks. A devotee—perhaps the donor—sits in reverence near her right foot, balanced by Sarasvati's animal mount, the gander (now headless), on the opposite side.

The inscription on the base records that an earlier sculpture of the goddess, dedicated to a Jain temple in 1069, was damaged in early 1152. The following year a nobleman named Parashurama commissioned the artist Jagadeva to create this replacement.

Ardhanarishvara, the Androgynous Form of Shiva and Parvati

Nepal, c. 1000

Cast copper with glass inlays

33 x 14 $^1\!/_2$ x 5 in. (83.8 x 36.8 x 12.7 cm)

From the Nasli and Alice Heeramaneck Collection, Museum Associates Purchase M.82.6.1

THIS EXTRAORDINARY IMAGE of Ardhanarishvara (lord who is half woman) depicts the combined forms of the Hindu god Shiva and his wife, Parvati. According to one myth, the Hindu god of creation, Brahma, neglected to create women; Shiva consequently transformed his left side into a woman. The two halves separated but ultimately recoupled to conceive humankind. On a domestic level, this combined form represents the ideal state of union between husband and wife, each representing one half of a whole. On a philosophical level, Shiva is the perfect yogi, or liberated being, who remains detached from the world while Parvati represents the creative energy that enlivens him. As such, the image symbolizes the inseparability of the male and female elements of existence.

Each half of the image has distinguishing physical features and clothing. Some aspects, such as the divided chest, are obvious references to gender, but other details, such as the wider arc of Parvati's hip, are more subtle. Parvati's tiara and elaborate coiffure contrast with Shiva's crown of matted hair, and the goddess's ankle-length garment differs from Shiva's knee-length wrap. Certain distinctions are more iconographic in character. Shiva's half face has a third eye in the forehead, and his raised hand holds a *vajra*, or thunderbolt, while Parvati holds an ascetic's water pot.

Brahma

Indonesia, central Java, c. 800–900

Andesite

45 ³/₄ x 17 ¹/₂ x 12 ¹/₂ in. (116.2 x 44.5 x 31.8 cm)

Gift of the 2000 Collectors Committee

M.2000.30

HINDUISM, UNLIKE BUDDHISM, did not spread from India to the entirety of Asia. The religion was, however, accepted in large parts of Southeast Asia, where it became associated with kingship and royal power. Hundreds of stone and brick Hindu temples were built in central Java between 750 and 950.

This consummate image of the Hindu god Brahma originally graced a niche in a Javanese temple. Traditionally portrayed as an ascetic, Brahma is shown here with a crownlike mound of twisted and matted hair, enriched by the jewels of the high born. His nature is also reflected in the two objects that flank him. The fire altar on the left, emitting a plume of scented smoke, refers to his role in Vedic (proto-Hindu) sacrifices, a practice continued by the Brahman priests of later India. The lobed water container on the right is one used by ascetics.

Brahma has four faces, one of which is hidden at the rear. His upper arms hold an honorific flywhisk (at right) and a circle of prayer beads with a flower (at left). The two empty hands in front of the body display unusual gestures, but may have once held a separate metal attribute, such as a bell.

Vishnu

Cambodia, Angkor, Pre Rup, Angkor period, c. 950

Sandstone

89 x 28 x 18 in. (226.1 x 71.1 x 45.7 cm)

Gift of Anna Bing Arnold

M.76.19

THIS IMPOSING SANDSTONE IMAGE of the Hindu god Vishnu once stood over nine feet tall, an expression of dominating sovereignty. The four arms originally spread outward from the enormous body, the great weight supported by the columnar legs. The concept was daring, but the arms that extended into space have since been lost.

The god wears a traditional Cambodian pleated garment, or *sampot*, which is a single piece of cloth wrapped around the waist, pulled up between the legs, and tucked into a belt at the back. Added pieces of cloth suspended from the belt at the front are arranged in a decorative manner dubbed "anchor folds" by Western art historians. Vishnu also wears an elaborate head ornament comprising a decorated diadem, with cloth ties knotted at the back, and a tiered crown surmounted by a jeweled knob. Both the *sampot* and headdress, marked by complex patterns, provide a strong contrast to the smooth surface of the polished, unadorned torso, thus amplifying the physical strength of the form.

Page from a Manuscript of the Qur'an

Tunisia, probably Qairawan, Fatimid dynasty, c. 850–950

Gold and red ink on parchment, dyed blue

11 1/8 x 14 3/4 in. (28.3 x 37.5 cm)

The Nasli M. Heeramaneck Collection, Gift of Joan Palevsky

M.86.196

ISLAM AROSE IN THE EARLY SEVENTH CENTURY under the leadership of the prophet Muhammad. It is the youngest of the world's three great monotheistic religions, following in the prophetic traditions of Judaism and Christianity. The Qur'an (meaning "recitation" in Arabic) is the holy book of Islam.

Calligraphy is the most highly esteemed Islamic art, perhaps because the act of writing transmits and preserves the Qur'an. Early Qur'ans were written in a type of angular script with letters rendered from right to left in broad horizontal strokes. This script was well suited to the oblong format of the parchment page. Parchment (also called vellum), made from cured and scraped animal skin, was the preferred material for Qur'ans up to the twelfth century, when it was replaced by paper.

Worthy of an imperial patron, this folio comes from a now partially dispersed Qur'an written in gold on blue parchment, perhaps dyed with indigo in emulation of Byzantine royal manuscripts and documents on purple vellum. It may belong to a seven-volume version described in a medieval inventory of the library of the Great Mosque in Qairawan (in modern Tunisia), where the book was most likely produced in the late ninth or early tenth century.

Lamp

Egypt or Syria, Mamluk dynasty,
c. 1350

Free-blown and tooled glass,
enameled and gilded

H. 13⅝ (34.6 cm)

William Randolph Hearst Collection
50.28.4

INSCRIPTIONS IN ISLAMIC ART were used to convey information and decorate surfaces. This beautiful lamp, embellished by rhythmic calligraphy and distinctive ornament, was most likely produced for a religious context. The neck of the lamp is inscribed with the first few words of a Qur'anic verse (xxiv.35) that likens the light of God to the light yielded by an oil lamp: "God is the Light of the heavens and of the earth."

Another inscription, located at the base of the lamp, indicates that this object was commissioned by Shaykhu al-Nasiri, whose heraldic emblem—a red cup set between a red and black bar—is repeated on the upper and lower sections of the lamp. This design refers to its owner's former status as a royal cup bearer. Shaykhu built a mosque and a *khanqa* (Sufi monastery) in Cairo in the mid-fourteenth century. Thus, this lamp was most likely made for one of these structures.

Tile with Scrolling Floral Arabesque

Greater Iran, Timurid dynasty, c. 1400–1500

Fritware, glazed and assembled as mosaic

$24\,^1/_4$ x $23\,^1/_2$ x $2\,^3/_4$ in. (61.6 x 59.7 x 7 cm)

The Madina Collection of Islamic Art, Gift of Camilla Chandler Frost

M.2002.1.19

THIS TILE BELONGS TO THE PERIOD of Timurid rule in Greater Iran (1370–1506). The Timurids were the last great dynasty to emerge from the Central Asian steppe. Their empire included modern Iran, Iraq, Afghanistan, parts of the Caucasus, and western Central Asia. Prodigious builders, the Timurids sponsored the construction of religious institutions and foundations that were often built on an enormous scale and commonly sheathed in an elaborate decorative skin of brilliant glazed tile.

In the greater Iranian world, the primary structural material was dun-colored baked brick; thus glazed tile provided colorful embellishment. The most complicated and time-consuming manner of fifteenth-century tile work was "mosaic faience." Elements of the floral design of the museum's tile were cut from glazed tiles of different colors and assembled as a mosaic. This tile was set in place on the exterior of a building, where it joined other tiles or panels as part of a larger, more complicated design.

Vessel with Dancing Women

Iran, Sasanian period, c. 500–700

Hammered silver with gilding

H. 6⅝ in. (16.8 cm)

Gift of Varya and Hans Cohn

AC1992.152.82

THE MUSEUM'S RICH COLLECTION of pre-Islamic Iranian metalwork includes early items cast in bronze, such as horse trappings and standard finials made in Luristan (1350–650 B.C.). Later objects such as this Sasanian vessel were not cast but hammered from a single piece of silver. The process was completed with repoussé decoration, raising in relief figures that were worked from the interior of the vessel. The addition of mercury gilding on the background emphasizes the three-dimensionality of the primary pattern.

A dozen or more examples from this period feature dancing females adorned with diadems, earrings, necklaces, bracelets, anklets, and flowing shawls. Scholars continue to debate whether the figures represent the Zoroastrian goddess Anahita—a votary of a vestigial cult of Dionysus—or a celebrant of a seasonal festival observed in Sasanian Iran.

CHINA AND THE SILK ROAD

The fabled Silk Road, a series of strategic highways and byways linking rich settlements and oases from western China to northern India and Iran, was used by missionaries and pilgrims propagating Buddhism and Islam. The same network also conveyed luxury goods across Asia. Chinese silks and ceramics reached the West in return for metalwork and glass. These imported luxuries profoundly influenced artistic traditions at both ends of Asia.

Flask with a Lion Attacking an Ox, China, late Six Dynasties period, Northern Zhou dynasty or Sui dynasty, 556–618, molded stoneware with incised decoration and green glaze, h. 12³⁄₈ in. (31.4 cm), given in memory of Dr. Joseph K. W. Li, AC1997.17.1

In China, trade objects inspired the exploration of new forms, motifs, and materials. An impressive flask (*bianhu*) in the museum's collection presents an almost unfiltered Chinese translation of pre-Islamic Sasanian Persian design. The ceramic vessel, now missing its shoulder lugs, must have been inspired by an imported leather or metal prototype. The two faces of the flattened clay form are covered with a stamped and carved narrative scene unlike anything found in earlier Chinese art. The image features three non-Chinese figures in foreign costume prodding an ox, lion, and cub engaged in violent combat. As the ox gores the lion with its horns, it is being bitten above and below by the lion and cub.

Exotic, imported forms first captivated Chinese consumers in the fifth and sixth centuries as interactions increased with

Jar, China, middle Tang dynasty, c. 700–800, mold-blown blue glass, h. 2 1/8 in. (5.4 cm), gift of Nicholas Grindley, M.2001.38

foreigners along the northwestern frontier. A brief introductory period marked by obvious copying of foreign models was followed by a much longer epoch in which Chinese artisans creatively adapted and reinterpreted Central, South, and West Asian types and explored new media such as glass and gilt silver. Thus, an attractive cosmetic box in the museum collection is decorated with phoenixes—a quintessential Chinese motif—and floral scrolls that provide only a hint of foreign inspiration.

Cosmetic or Medicine Box in the Form of a Clamshell, China, middle Tang dynasty, c. 700–800, hammered silver with chased and partially gilded decoration, 1 1/2 x 3 1/8 x 3 in. (3.8 x 7.9 x 7.6 cm), purchased with funds provided by members of the Far Eastern Art Council, M.2000.57

Jar

Japan, Aichi prefecture, Kamakura period, c. 1200–1400

Tokoname ware; coil-built stoneware with ash glaze

H. 17 1/4 in. (43.8 cm)

Purchased with funds provided by the Museum Associates, the Frederick R. Weisman Company, and the Far Eastern Art Council

M.80.77

THIS MASSIVE ASYMMETRICAL STORAGE or shipping jar has a broad shoulder and narrow foot, exuding strength and solidity. Placed unglazed in kilns, such pieces were fired for up to two weeks. In the high heat, the body, rich in iron, turned a vibrant red. Flying wood ash settled on the surface, liquefied, and created rivulets of what is called a natural or ash glaze.

Large, robust containers were made throughout the country to serve local needs. They can be linked to specific kilns by their distinctive clay body, repertoire of shapes, and surface designs. The chestnut-red body and greenish flowing glaze are typical of the assertive coil-built forms and natural ash glazes of pots made at Tokoname, in the southwest of present-day Aichi prefecture.

Incense Burner in the Form of an Ancient Bronze Container

China, Hebei Province, Quyang County, middle or late Northern Song dynasty, c. 1000–1127
Ding ware; wheel-thrown stoneware with applied decoration and transparent glaze
H. 4 1/2 in. (11.4 cm)

Purchased with funds provided by the Far Eastern Art Council in celebration of the new Chinese Galleries
AC1998.90.1

THE BURNING OF SPECIALLY PREPARED mixtures of woods and other vegetal matter acquired great popularity in China by the Song dynasty (960–1279). In palaces, temples, and scholars' retreats, the infusion of fragrant scents transported mere mortals to a higher meditative plane. The incense burner (*lu*) was an essential element in the practice.

This ivory-toned example embodies the aesthetic sophistication of Northern Song (960–1127) ceramic production. Its elegant yet simple shape—a wide cylinder encircled by pairs of raised lines set on three delicate feet—was formed of very fine white clay. The vessel is covered in the smooth, clear glaze typical of wares from the Ding kilns in northern China. Only the rim is unglazed, allowing the incense burner to be placed

upside down in the kiln during firing to protect its form from collapsing. A silver or bronze band, now lost, would have covered the unglazed rim and guarded against chipping.

Subtle Ding wares, produced both for the palace and for the general market, reflect the aesthetic refinement of China's most discriminating audiences—the imperial household and the urbanized, highly educated civil servant class. The form of this incense burner, based on an ancient bronze *lian* vessel first popular in the Han dynasty (206 B.C.–A.D. 220), further illustrates the elite interest in antiquities fashionable during the Song dynasty.

Oval Tray with Pavilion on a Garden Terrace

China, Yuan dynasty, 1279–1368

Carved red lacquer on wood

9 1/4 x 6 3/8 in. (23.5 x 16.2 cm)

Gift of Mr. and Mrs. John H. Nessley

M.81.125.1

THIS SMALL TRAY FEATURES a detailed scene of two scholars relaxing on a garden terrace. In the pavilion, an attendant watches his master nod over a laden table. On the terrace, a servant carries a musical instrument while following the second scholar on his way home. The natural forms, architectural details, furnishings, and figures were derived from painted narratives, while the stylized conventions of rosettes and meanders were likely influenced by textile design.

The tray is a remarkable example of the pictorial qualities of Yuan dynasty carved lacquer, which displayed amazing visual depth on small, flat surfaces. This time-consuming method of construction and decoration involved building up lacquer, one thin layer at a time, over a wooden core to form a strong and stable medium for carving. By the Yuan period, the technique was treated with the lapidarian expertise, superior skill, and precise control usually reserved for other luxury materials such as jade and ivory.

Jar with Peony Sprays and Lotuses

Korea, late Koryŏ dynasty, c. 1200–1392

Wheel-thrown and shaped stoneware with carved and slip-covered ground and glaze-painted decoration

H. 11 1/2 in. (29.2 cm)

Purchased with Museum Funds

M.2000.15.87

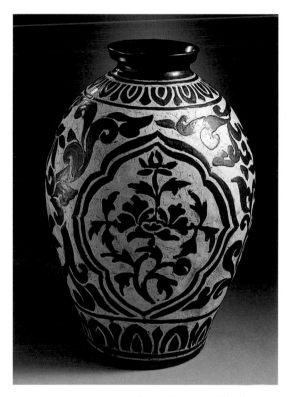

DURING THE KORYŎ DYNASTY, Korean potters developed extremely complex methods of adding color to the surface of their wares. This jar illustrates one of the most laborious approaches. Exemplified by only a few surviving examples worldwide, the technique may have been restricted to select pieces made at special kilns for the exclusive use of the Korean court. The process, resulting in bold floral patterns rendered in a rich brown glaze on an unglazed ground, involved a series of steps. Like the few other rare survivors, the wheel-thrown form was gently pressed from front and back, producing a flattened field for decoration. The primary motifs— peony sprays, cusped frames, lotus scrolls, and lotus petal borders—were brushed in ink. The surface surrounding the sketched patterns was scraped away and covered with a buff-colored clay wash. The inked designs were then covered with an iron-rich glaze and fired. The intense heat of the kiln set the oily brown glaze and produced a light-colored biscuit—or unglazed surface—marked by an intricate web of cracks.

Ewer with Figures

Iran, Kashan, early medieval, c. 1200–1230

Fritware, overglaze painted (*mina'i*)

H. 13 in. (33 cm)

The Madina Collection of Islamic Art, Gift of Camilla Chandler Frost

M.2002.1.7

IRANIAN POTTERS FROM THE CITY OF KASHAN introduced a polychromatic decorative technique called *mina'i* (Persian for "enamel") for luxury ceramics. This type of multicolored ornamentation was produced in a complicated process that required at least two firings. Vessels were first covered with an opaque white or a turquoise glaze and fired. After the initial firing, additional decoration, painted in enamel colors (including red, black, and white), was applied on top of the glaze. The added colors were fixed in a second firing at a lower temperature.

Unlike some *mina'i* wares that illustrate scenes from the Iranian national epic, the *Shahnama* (Book of kings), the museum's ewer features elaborate decoration that defies identification. Delicately painted horsemen occupy the

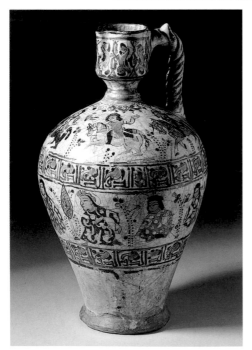

upper register, while seated courtiers, a musician, and perhaps a dancer appear in the lower band. Together, the motifs seem to represent "the good life." Apparently, *mina'i* ware was not produced after the early thirteenth century, yet it is one of the best known and most popular types of medieval Iranian ceramics among collectors today.

**Foliated Platter with the
Eight Buddhist Symbols**

China, Jiangxi Province,
Jingdezhen, late Yuan dynasty,
c. 1340–68

Molded porcelain with blue
painted decoration under
clear glaze

Diam. 17³⁄₄ in. (45.1 cm)

Gift of the Francis E. Fowler, Jr., Foundation
and Los Angeles County Fund

55.40

FOLLOWING THE ADVENT OF
successful porcelain production,
Chinese potters began to explore new decorative possibilities. Inspired by
Iranian practices, they painted mineral pigments directly on clay surfaces
before coating the vessels with a clear vitreous glaze and firing them. By
the fourteenth century, the Chinese porcelain industry, located in the
southeastern province of Jiangxi, was creating extremely attractive wares
enriched with deep blue patterns brushed in cobalt imported from Iran.
Such blue-and-whites proved popular both at home and abroad, with trade
facilitated by the Mongol domination of most of Asia.

Although this massive platter with a flat, foliated rim conforms to the
shape and scale of vessels used in the Islamic countries of western Asia,
the presence of ornamental motifs favored by the Chinese suggests that it
was likely made for the domestic market. A feathery wave pattern
accentuates the rim and covers the inner wall, which is also highlighted by
six cusped frames enclosing lotuses, morning glories, and melons, plants
and flowers popular in Chinese painting. The center of the platter is painted
with pie-shaped segments containing the eight Buddhist symbols indicative
of auspicious wishes.

The extraordinary popularity of Chinese porcelains throughout Asia and
Europe continued into the subsequent Ming (1368–1644) and Qing
(1644–1911) dynasties and influenced ceramic production worldwide.

Jar with Dragon and Clouds

Korea, probably Kwangju, South Chŏlla Province, late Chosŏn period,
c. 1700–1800

Wheel-thrown porcelain with blue painted decoration under clear glaze

H. 17 1/2 in. (44.5 cm)

Purchased with Museum Funds

M.2000.15.98

PORCELAINS WITH UNDERGLAZE designs painted in blue were first produced in Korea during the fifteenth century when native sources of cobalt were discovered. The relatively high iron content of Korean cobalt yielded a somewhat muddy color, however, leading local artisans to prefer minerals imported to Korea through China from Iran. Due to the high cost of the foreign pigment, only the royal household was initially entitled to use the precious wares. In the eighteenth century, however, when Korea entered an age of prosperity and renewed cultural activity, blue-and-whites were available to a broader range of society.

Many porcelains were produced in the late eighteenth century at the government-controlled kilns in Kwangju, near the Chosŏn capital of Hanyang (modern Seoul). Court painters were frequently employed to paint the surface designs. This robust, elegant jar features a scaly dragon with big friendly eyes, sharp teeth, small horns, and a lively mane. Considered auspicious throughout East Asia, the dragon symbolizes royalty and prosperity. This boldly painted creature attests to the brush of a skillful court artist and anticipates later decorative trends in court and folk painting.

Jar with Floral Scrolls

Turkey, Iznik, Ottoman period, c. 1500–1510

Fritware, underglaze painted

H. 9 1/2 in. (24.1 cm)

The Edwin Binney, 3rd Turkish Collection

M.85.237.80

CHINESE CERAMICS WERE LONG ADMIRED, collected, and emulated in the Islamic world, especially at the Ottoman court in Istanbul. Chinese blue-and-whites proved particularly popular, influencing the development of Iznik ware, named after the city in northwestern Anatolia where the type was made. It is one of the most representative of Ottoman arts, comprising architectural decoration as well as tableware. The type has a hard, dense, artificial clay body that was covered with a brilliant white slip replicating the effect of Chinese porcelains. The surface—embellished with floral scrolls, arabesques, and other designs in deep cobalt blue—was ultimately covered with a shiny, colorless glaze.

This superb Iznik jar is decorated with dynamic floral patterns of Chinese inspiration painted in two shades of blue. The flowers appear

variously on a white ground or reserved against blue. Jars of this type were most likely used as storage containers and exemplify the high aesthetic standards of the day.

Ardabil Carpet

Iran, Safavid dynasty, dated 1539–40

Knotted wool pile on silk foundation

283 x 157 1/2 in. (718.8 x 400.1 cm)

Gift of J. Paul Getty

53.50.2

AMONG THE WORLD'S MOST FAMOUS works of art, this carpet and its mate in the Victoria and Albert Museum in London were products of the great flowering of the arts under the Safavid dynasty of Iran (1501–1732). The carpets were probably royal gifts to the shrine at Ardabil in northwest Iran, a site sacred to the dynasty's Shi'ite rulers. Both carpets (made in a royal textile workshop, perhaps the one at Tabriz) are signed and dated early in the reign of Shah Tahmasp (reigned 1524–76), a renowned arts patron. Each carpet features the same inscription, including a couplet by the fourteenth-century poet Hafiz: "Other than thy threshold I have no refuge in this world. / My head has no resting place other than this doorway. / Work of a servant of the court, Maqsud of Kashan [in] the year 946 [1539–40]." Maqsud was most likely the designer or production supervisor, not the weaver.

The museum's carpet contains 15.5 million asymmetrical knots (approximately 350 to the square inch) and may have taken three or four weavers, working simultaneously, more than four years to complete. A large central medallion with a field of overlapping floral arabesques dominates the carpet's intricate design. This focal point is surrounded by sixteen lobed medallions and flanked by a pair of lamps on the carpet's longer axis.

Nushirvan Receives an Embassy from the Khaqan

Iran, Tabriz, Safavid dynasty, c. 1530–35

Ink, opaque watercolor, and gold on paper

18⅝ x 12⅝ in. (47.3 x 32.1 cm)

Gift of the 1989 Collectors Committee

M.89.55

THIS PAINTING COMES FROM A MANUSCRIPT whose size, scale, and quality make it one of the most luxurious Islamic books ever created. Now dispersed, the *Shahnama* (Book of kings) was made for Shah Tahmasp (reigned 1524–76) in Tabriz, the capital of the Safavid dynasty at the time. The manuscript originally included 258 illustrations, hundreds of illuminations, and more than one thousand pages of text, all with gold-flecked borders. A book of this magnitude probably took several years to complete.

The museum's illustration, with its rich colors and patterns, contrived landscape, and gold sky, depicts a perfect world—a most suitable, if

unreal, setting for a royal audience. In *Shahnama* illustrations, kings, heroes, and courtly figures are depicted as idealized types with features that reflect the ethnicity of the ruling elite. This identification between ancient Iranian kings and contemporary rulers was deliberate and significant. The arts of the book were often employed to further political agendas and to justify and legitimize the ruling elite.

Attributed to **Abu'l Hasan** (India, born 1588/89, active c. 1600–1635)
Emperor Jahangir Triumphing over Poverty, c. 1622
Ink, opaque watercolor, and gold on paper
9³/₈ x 6 in. (23.8 x 15.2 cm)
From the Nasli and Alice Heeramaneck Collection, Museum Associates Purchase
M.75.4.28

THIS PAINTING IS ONE OF A NUMBER of allegorical works devised to project the Mughal emperor Jahangir (reigned 1605–27) as a just ruler. At this time the emperor was preoccupied with civil unrest and a rebellion led by his son. The work is attributed to Abu'l Hasan, a highly favored court artist. The inscription in the upper right conveys the artist's intentions: "An auspicious portrait of his exalted majesty, who by the arrow of generosity eradicated the trace of Daliddar—the very personification of poverty—from the world and laid the foundation for a new world with his justice and munificence."

Jahangir shoots an arrow into an emaciated old man who represents poverty. The two cherubs holding the crown above the emperor indicate his divine right to rule. In the upper left corner, another cherub holds an ornamented chain reaching from heaven to earth, a sign of Jahangir's commitment to implementing God's justice. Other symbols suggest the larger geopolitical context that confronted Jahangir. The emperor stands on a lion that straddles the globe, a symbol of the Mughal empire; the lion lies peacefully beside a smaller lamb that represents Safavid Iran. Although the depiction suggests that harmony existed between the two empires, they were, in reality, political and commercial rivals. The globe also functions as a nimbus for Manu, the Hindu lawgiver whose presence reflects the Hindu populace, which constituted the majority of Jahangir's subjects.

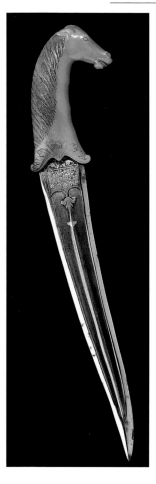

Dagger of Emperor Aurangzeb

India, Mughal, dated 1660–61

Nephrite jade and steel inlaid with gold

13³⁄₄ x 2 in. (34.9 x 5.1 cm)

From the Nasli and Alice Heeramaneck Collection, Museum Associates Purchase
M.76.2.7a

MUGHAL JADE WORKING was the most demanding and accomplished form of sculptural expression in northern India from the seventeenth to the mid-nineteenth century. An extremely tough stone, jade can be shaped only through abrasion and polishing rather than carving.

This dagger is a stunning example of the ornate ceremonial weapons described as favored imperial objects in the *Ma'āsir-i 'Ālamgīrī* (The Illustrious acts of Alamgir), the official court chronicle of the Mughal emperor Aurangzeb (reigned 1658–1707). An inscription inlaid in gold on the watered steel blade dates the dagger 1660–61 and, along with the symbolic royal parasol, certifies that it was made for the emperor himself.

A technical tour de force that also closely approximates the natural world, the pale green nephrite hilt is fashioned in the form of a spirited horse's head with delicately rendered ears, high cheekbones, open lips, and precisely detailed teeth. The mane is colored burnt orange and represents the use of the naturally occurring iron-stained rind of the stone. The neck of the horse is gently rippled, making the hilt easier to hold. Aurangzeb spent much of his life on horseback in battle or hunting. He particularly cherished his mounts and gave them honorific names such as "Agile as the Wind." The emperor similarly named his favorite daggers and swords with epithets such as "World Conqueror."

Ewer with Dragon Handle

China, Ming dynasty, probably Jiajing period, 1522–66

Carved black and red lacquer on wood

H. 11 $^{7}/_{16}$ in. (29 cm)

Gift of Dale and Nicole Lum

AC1998.222.1

DURING THE SIXTEENTH CENTURY in China, ewers with long narrow spouts, arched handles, and peach-shaped cartouches were made in a variety of materials, including gold, silver, cloisonné enamel, lacquer, and porcelain. Many of the porcelain examples were exported and still exist in collections in western Asia and Japan, especially Okinawa. Carved lacquer ewers are far more rare, presumably due to their limited production and fragility.

Despite its somewhat exotic shape, this ewer features elaborately carved decoration that was particularly meaningful to a Chinese audience. Deer, mythical single-horned *qilin*, and auspicious emblems allude to wealth, virtue, and professional accomplishment. The fish spout-strut and dragon handle represent success in the civil service exams. A scholar's

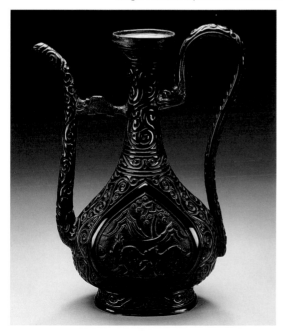

endurance throughout the grueling examination process was compared to a carp swimming upstream. The ultimate reward of official appointment was symbolized by the transformation of the fish into a dragon. Undoubtedly, the ewer was made to honor a scholar-official and may have been used in special court-initiated celebrations.

Xiang Shengmo (China, 1592–1658)

Beckoning of Solitude (detail), dated 1626

Handscroll; ink on paper

11 1/2 x 300 in. (29.2 x 762 cm)

Los Angeles County Fund

60.29.2

THIS PAINTING, ABOUT TWENTY-FIVE FEET LONG, depicts an intimate journey in the life of a recluse. The delicate details transport the viewer along solitary mountain paths to rocky caverns and open fields. In his inscription, the painter Xiang Shengmo writes that he took nine months to complete the painting because he could work only at night, when he was freed from other responsibilities.

Born to an eminent family in the Jiangnan region of south China during the waning years of the Ming dynasty (1368–1644), Xiang had a privileged upbringing in the household of his grandfather Xiang Yuanbian, a prominent art collector. The deft and practiced brushwork owes much to Xiang Shengmo's study of ancient masterworks in his family's collection. As the

scroll is unrolled, it reveals groves of trees and rocky outcrops of almost abstract formations, recalling the work of Dong Qichang, a family friend who was the foremost scholar-official, painter-calligrapher, and art critic of his day. Dong mentored Xiang during the creation of this painting and wrote the title and an inscription (following the image) in running script applauding Xiang's accomplishments.

Shitao (China, 1642–1707)

Landscape, dated 1694

Leaf from an 8-leaf album; ink and color on paper

11 x 8³/₄ in. (27.9 x 22.2 cm)

Los Angeles County Fund

60.29.1d

SHITAO, DESCENDED FROM the Ming imperial house, was born Zhu Ruoji. In 1644, when Manchurian forces overthrew the Ming and founded the Qing dynasty (1644–1911), a retainer saved young Zhu from death and found refuge for him in a series of Buddhist temples. Henceforth, Zhu was known by the Buddhist name Yuanji Shitao, or simply Shitao.

As a monk-artist, Shitao traveled widely, meeting artists, poets, and even nobles at court. His views on painting and calligraphy often disagreed with conventional practices. He defended his work, stating, "I use my own method." His individualism is evident in his varied painting styles and awkward calligraphy.

In the 1690s, Shitao left the Buddhist faith to become a Daoist, whereupon he worked as an artist in Yangzhou, an affluent commercial city on the southeast coast. This painting is from an album of eight leaves painted in Yangzhou. Shitao inscribed most of the images with melancholic poems about wilderness, rain, personal failure, and aging. He dated the last leaf 1694. Shitao's poem (translated by Jonathan Hay) at the lower right despondently questions his aimless wandering and confronts the feelings of loneliness that accompany the end of life's journey: "Who shares one's vicissitudes in the world? / In my old age I have no possessions, and have turned crazy and stubborn."

Pyŏn Sangbyŏk (Korea, active c. 1750–85)

Portrait of Scholar-Official Yun Ponggu in His Seventieth Year, dated 1750

Hanging scroll; ink and color on silk

46 3/4 x 35 in. (118.7 x 88.9 cm)

Purchased with Museum Funds

M.2000.15.17

PRODUCED AS LARGE HANGING SCROLLS or smaller album images, portraits in Confucian Korea usually showed a single subject in formal dress. Many of the scrolls were made for display in government buildings, where they honored learning, individual accomplishment, and public service. Others were preserved for generations in private academies of learning or clan ancestral halls. Treated as treasured institutional or family possessions, they were hung on special days when the spirit and success of the deceased were celebrated according to established ritual customs.

This portrait scroll is ascribed to a well-known artist of the Royal Painting

Bureau, Pyŏn Sangbyŏk. Here, he illustrates his subject in an informal robe and hat, seated on a woven floor mat in an extremely spare setting. The title identifies the sitter as Yun Ponggu (1681–1767) at seventy years of age. Yun passed the national civil service examination in 1714 but was stripped of official rank after an intrigue at court in 1741. Reinstated the following year, he was ultimately appointed chief of one of the six boards of the Chosŏn government and lived out a respected career.

KOREAN COURT PAINTING

The Korean court established a royal painting bureau during the fifteenth century. The bureau employed approximately forty artists, including fifteen students selected by examination. Often several generations of the same family worked as court artists. Members of the bureau worked on a variety of official projects, including portraits, Confucian book illustrations, architectural decoration, porcelain designs, and military maps. Documentary and decorative screens made for various palace buildings were particularly significant assignments.

One important court screen in the museum's collection commemorates the sixtieth birthday of the Dowager Queen Sinjŏng (1808–1890). Lady Cho, as she was called before becoming a member of the royal family, had married a crown prince when she was only eleven years old. Sadly, her young husband died before ascending the throne. The dowager queen also outlived her son, King Hŏnjong (reigned 1834–49). Thus, when she celebrated her sixtieth birthday in 1868, a more distant descendant had succeeded to the throne.

Sixtieth Birthday Banquets for Dowager Queen Sinjŏng (detail), dated 1868, Korea, end of the Chosŏn period, 8-panel screen, ink, color, and gold on silk, 53 x 144 in. (134.6 x 365.8 cm), purchased with Museum Funds, M.2000.15.35

Sixtieth Birthday Banquets for Dowager Queen Sinjŏng features scenes from three different ceremonies held within the Kyŏngbok Palace in Seoul. The unusual style of the screen can be traced to earlier Chinese traditions of illustrating ritual events. In the illustrated detail, which shows one ceremony, women perform elaborate dances in the tented forecourt of the main audience hall. Inside the hall, another group of palace ladies conducts ceremonial acts in front of an empty throne backed

"Elegant Gathering in the Western Garden," Korea, late Chosŏn period, c. 1700–1800, 10-panel screen, ink and color on silk, 63 x 144 in. (160 x 365.8 cm), purchased with Museum Funds, M.2000.15.30

by a screen showing royal symbols—the sun and moon above five sacred peaks—that represent the king's presence, even though he is not shown.

Painted screens are also depicted in another court-commissioned work in the museum's collection. Unlike *Sixtieth Birthday Banquets for Dowager Queen Sinjŏng, "Elegant Gathering in the Western Garden"* portrays the fictional meeting of famous Chinese scholars and statesmen of the eleventh century. Within a large walled garden, various figures in Chinese scholars' robes engage in the leisurely pastimes of painting, calligraphy, poetry, and music. This subject was particularly popular among the educated civil servants who staffed the Korean government. Although based on Chinese models, this rendition, like other examples signed by Korean court painters, shows creative adaptations and the characteristic use of a large-format folding screen.

Quail amid Autumn Grasses and Flowers

Japan, Momoyama period, 1573–1615

6-panel screen; ink, color, and gold leaf on paper

68³/₄ x 141 in. (174.6 x 358.1 cm)

Gift of Julia and Leo Krashen in honor of the tenth anniversary of the Pavilion for Japanese Art

AC1999.223.1

ELEGANT PAINTINGS OF QUAIL with autumn grasses and flowers are a trademark subject of the Tosa School, a group of painters who worked primarily for the imperial Japanese court. The school flourished from the sixteenth to the nineteenth century, creating works with delicate lines, meticulous details, and a lavish use of expensive mineral pigments.

This Tosa screen depicts highly realistic quail and plants on a gold-leaf decorative ground, resulting in a stunning contrast between painstaking detail and abstract flattened space. The composition is dominated by the delicately curved blades of autumn grasses, with pale stalks of golden

pampas grass beyond. Flowers appropriate to the season—blue gentians, field chrysanthemums, and boneset—are subtly sprinkled across the surface. A number of quail hide among the plants, three feeling secure enough to fall asleep.

A folding screen could be used as a room divider or privacy screen and is equally effective viewed under diffuse daylight or when seen at night by candlelight.

Ogata Kenzan (Japan, 1663–1743)

The Twelfth Month from Plates of the Twelve Months (detail)

Slab-built stoneware with underglaze blue and black, clear glaze, and overglaze painted enamel decoration

8 x 7 x ½ in. (20.3 x 17.8 x 1.3 cm)

Purchased with funds provided by the Japan Business Association and the Far Eastern Art Council

M.84.64.12

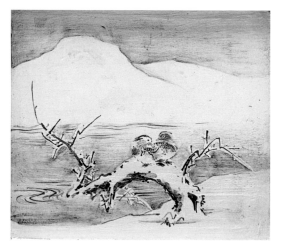

OGATA KENZAN WAS THE FIRST highly educated and cultivated Japanese artist-merchant to operate a ceramic workshop. He created a new style of painterly wares exemplified here by a rare, intact set of twelve seasonal dishes originally intended for food presentation in the tea ceremony.

The top, bottom, and sides of each plate are enriched with brushed embellishment. The upper surfaces, painted in delicate tones, feature landscape vignettes appropriate to specific months. The images are inspired by the poetry of the nobleman Fujiwara no Teika. Composed in 1214, the lines have been written by Kenzan on the bottom of the plates. Pale cobalt-blue wisteria patterns ornament the outer walls.

The twelfth plate from the set is decorated with a painting of mandarin ducks floating on a frigid pond. The poem reads: "Mandarin Ducks / The snow falls on the ice of the pond / On which I gaze; / Piling up, as does this passing year, on all those passed / And on the feathered coat of the mandarin duck, / The 'bird of regret.'"

Hanging Flower Vase in the Form of a Quiver

Japan, Saga prefecture, Edo period, Enpŏ-Kyŏhŏ eras, 1673–1736

Nabeshima ware; slab-built porcelain with molded, modeled, cut, and incised decoration, and celadon glaze

14 1/2 x 7 in. (36.8 x 17.8 cm)

Gift of the 1995 Collectors Committee

AC1995.55.1

THIS HANGING FLOWER VASE was displayed in the center of a *tokonoma*, or art alcove, a place of honor in a traditional Japanese room. Inspired by the shape of a fourteenth-century leather quiver, it evokes the samurai warrior values of bravery, endurance, and loyalty. It might have been used only once a year, on the Boys' Day Festival held on the fifth day of the fifth month in the lunar calendar, when irises are in full bloom. On this day, families celebrated the warrior virtues and hoped their sons would embody them. The only known intact example of its kind, this vase

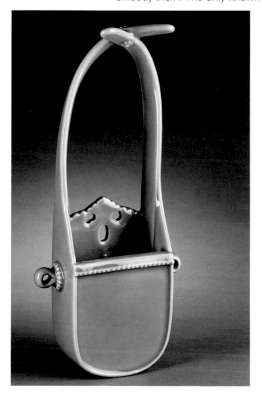

matches a fragment excavated at Ōkawachi, an early-eighteenth-century Nabeshima kiln.

Nabeshima porcelains were produced in present-day Saga prefecture in southern Japan. They are unrivaled in their abstract designs, delicate forms, and pure glaze colors. The Nabeshima kilns were under the exclusive control of the ruling *daimyō* (local lord), who either used the wares himself or gave them as gifts to other feudal lords. They were not made for sale. Production was closely supervised, technical secrets were carefully guarded, and less-than-perfect pieces were destroyed. The result was an extremely limited number of porcelains of superb quality

Katsushika Hokusai (Japan, 1760–1849)

South Wind, Clear Dawn from Thirty-six Views of Mount Fuji, c. 1830–31

Color woodblock print

10 x 14³⁄₈ in. (25.4 x 36.5 cm)

Gift of the Frederick R. Weisman Company

M.81.91.1

THIS PRINT, OFTEN CALLED *RED FUJI*, is the greatest design of Hokusai's best-known series, Thirty-six Views of Mount Fuji. The series, eventually comprising forty-six views, featured the most famous landmark of Japan in all seasons, scenic variations, and atmospheric conditions.

South Wind, Clear Dawn is the only print in the series that shows the mountain without human figures. The tense asymmetry of the composition results from three colors and a single outline, the product of Hokusai's long study and experimentation with form. This is a spectacular impression of this celebrated print, its colors retaining their original vibrancy. Hokusai's works had a deep and lasting effect not only on Japanese art but also on modern Western art.

Mochizuki Hanzan [Haritsu II] (Japan, active c. 1750–1800)

Stationery Box with Pheasant

Wood with lacquer and various inlays, including pottery, mother-of-pearl, horn, lead, pewter, and stag antler

$4\,{}^{1}/_{2}$ x $10\,{}^{1}/_{8}$ x $11\,{}^{7}/_{8}$ in. (11.4 x 25.7 x 30.2 cm)

Purchased with funds provided by the Far Eastern Art Council and friends of Virginia Atchley in honor of her ninetieth birthday

M.2002.4a–b

THIS STATIONERY BOX, created from a spectacular piece of heavily knotted cedar or male mulberry wood, features a variety of inlay materials and lacquer techniques. The maker, Mochizuki Hanzan, was inspired by Ogawa Haritsu (1663–1747), an earlier master of inlay and three-dimensional effects in lacquer design. Haritsu, in turn, had looked to the Rimpa School of painters, potters, and lacquer makers for inspiration.

The lid features a horned pheasant amid ferns and flowers associated with early spring. The pheasant is a symbol of nobility; when paired with spring plants it signifies richness and plenty. The design continues around the sides of the box. The interior, decorated by an unknown lacquer artist about one hundred years after the completion of the outside, features a silver-and-gold design of crows and a cherry tree on a windy day. The

realistic depiction of the blossoming cherry is enriched by the dark silhouettes of the crows on the modulated silver and gold–streaked background.

NETSUKE: TREASURES IN MINIATURE

Kimono, the traditional form of Japanese dress, had no pockets. A woman could tuck small items into her sleeves, but men, wearing a differently designed garment, chose to hang portable personal effects from a cord attached to the sash of the robe. A small toggle, called a *netsuke*, was used to keep the cord from slipping through the sash.

Because netsuke were intended to function in this way, they were necessarily small and compact. Most were made of ivory or wood, but other durable materials—including stag antler, glass, porcelain, stoneware, cloisonné enamel, lacquer, and amber— were also used. Netsuke were always carved to hang naturally and show their best side. Craftsmen worked within these restrictions to depict subjects that evoked the interests of their patrons as well as favorite historical, mythological, genre, or natural themes.

Although the earliest netsuke date from the seventeenth century, the art form matured in the eighteenth and first half of the nineteenth century, spawning a vast number of themes and styles. As Western men's clothing increasingly replaced kimono at the end of the nineteenth century, the purchasing of netsuke became primarily an activity of connoisseurs. Ironically, some of the finest examples were made after netsuke ceased to be objects of everyday use.

The museum's Bushell Collection displays a nearly encyclopedic array of works from various periods, carvers, locales, and materials. Signature pieces include *Dancing Fox*, who turns into a coquettish woman to seduce travelers and monks; *Bundle of Firewood*, carved from a single block of wood by Sōko; and a superb rendering of *Baku*, the legendary animal who eats nightmares.

Sōko [Morita Kisaburō] (Japan, 1879–1943), *Bundle of Firewood*, boxwood, 1 15/16 x 1 1/4 x 1 in. (4.9 x 3.2 x 2.5 cm), Raymond and Frances Bushell Collection, M.90.186.12

Dancing Fox, Japan, Edo period, c. 1700–1800, ivory with dark staining and *sumi* (ink), 2 13/16 x 1 1/16 x 15/16 in. (7.1 x 2.7 x 2.3 cm), Raymond and Frances Bushell Collection, AC1998.249.69

Attributed to Gechū (Japan, active 18th century), *Baku*, ivory with staining, *sumi* (ink), and traces of red pigment, 3 3/4 x 1 5/8 x 1 3/16 in. (9.5 x 4.1 x 3.0 cm), Raymond and Frances Bushell Collection, AC1998.249.63

Moriguchi Kakō (Japan, born 1909)

Kun'en, dated 1968

Paste-resist dyeing on silk crepe

$63\,^{7}/_{16}$ x $50\,^{13}/_{16}$ in. (161 X 129 cm)

Gift of the 1999 Collectors Committee

AC1999.113.1

KYOTO TEXTILE ARTIST MORIGUCHI KAKŌ revitalized the traditional paste-resist dyeing technique known as *yūzen* and was designated a "Living National Treasure" by the Japanese government in 1967. Developed during the Genroku era (1688–1704) of the Edo period (1615–1868), *yūzen* permitted the direct application of dyes on silk with a brush. This revolutionary technique helped to establish kimono as a highly respected format for Japanese artists.

Moriguchi created *Kun'en* (Fragrant garden) in 1968 at the height of his career. This "wearable painting" is embellished with a single chrysanthemum blossom that dramatically covers the entire surface of the kimono. The petals gradually increase in length and width as the blossom spirals and swirls to the outer limits of the garment. Each petal was precisely drawn with pale blue water-soluble ink (*aobana*) and then painstakingly outlined with a rice paste. The blue ink was then washed away, and each petal was filled with rice paste to reserve it in white while dyes were brushed on, a process allowing no room for error. Within the interstices of the petals, Moriguchi employed his signature *makinori* (scatter paste) technique, a lost process that he successfully reinvented. It adds an effervescent effect that gives depth to the overall design. Because of these meticulous procedures, the garment took almost five months to complete. The final result is an extremely refined kimono, at once traditional and contemporary.

EUROPEAN ART

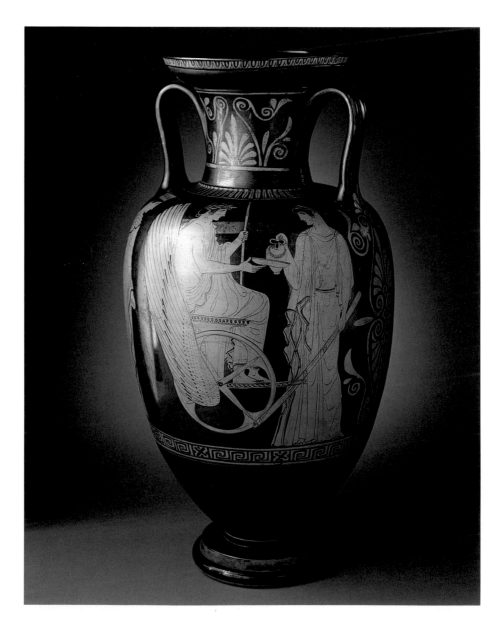

Red-Figure Neck-Amphora with Libation of Triptolemos

Attributed to the Hector Painter

Greece, Attica, c. 440–430 B.C.

Ceramic

H. 19 $^1/_4$ in. (49 cm); diam. 10 $^1/_8$ in. (25.8 cm)

William Randolph Hearst Collection

50.8.23

THE FINEST GREEK VASES were produced in the fifth century B.C., when this amphora was made, and can be attributed to a variety of artists. Based on the style of draftsmanship, this vase is one of approximately a dozen works attributed to the Hector Painter. The designation derives from the artist's identifying piece, or "name vase," depicting the departure of Hector, the legendary son of King Priam of Troy, which is now in the collection of the Vatican. Originally designed to serve as a wine container or decanter, the amphora is painted in the red-figure style, which was adopted around 530 B.C. and rapidly superseded the black-figure style.

According to myth, the goddess Demeter chose the demigod Triptolemos to travel the world and teach the Greeks the skills of agriculture. Briefly represented on Attic vases as a man seated on a cart, Triptolemos was depicted by 440 B.C. as a heroic youth riding in a heavenly chariot, serving as a symbol of the civility of the Athenian world. This vase shows Triptolemos receiving a libation from Persephone, daughter of Demeter, who lowers her long torch in a gesture of homage and pours wine from a spouted vessel into his *phiale* (shallow drinking bowl). Demeter stands behind him, bearing a sheaf of wheat and wearing a *polos* on her head, symbols of fecundity. On the reverse side of the amphora, a woman (possibly a priestess) extends a *phiale* to two youths, perhaps a worldly enactment of the mythological scene.

ANCIENT EGYPT

In addition to works of art that fall neatly within the broad cate-
gories of this book—Asian, European, Latin American, American,
and Modern and Contemporary art—LACMA possesses significant holdings from the continent of Africa. These include works
from the ancient civilization of Egypt, Islamic centers, and the
more recent traditional cultures of the sub-Saharan regions of
the continent. Two objects from the
Egyptian collection are described here,
complementing the Classical works of
art in this section.

Round-Topped Stela of Iuf-er-bak
depicts an Eighteenth Dynasty Egyptian
noble and members of his family
participating in a funerary banquet.
More banqueters appear in the register
below. The figures, rendered in delicate,
shallow relief, are shown in the composite perspective favored by ancient
Egyptian artists. In this method, figures
are represented through a combination
of frontal and profile views. Although
well aware of more sophisticated
drawing techniques, Egyptian artists
believed that simultaneously displaying
multiple points of view provided the most complete and definitive
record of the subject. Here, the eyes are shown frontally, defined
by beautifully preserved carved double lines and pigment
indicating the pupils. Originally, the entire surface was painted,
and traces of pigment are still visible in the wigs and hieroglyphic
texts. The stela, which was placed within a tomb as a permanent
monument and a request for perpetual offerings, reminded
visitors of the achievements of the tomb owner.

Round-Topped Stela of Iuf-er-bak,
Egypt, mid-18th Dynasty, c. 1391–
1353 B.C., limestone, 26 3/4 x 17 1/4 in.
(67.9 x 43.8 cm), purchased with funds
provided by Phil Berg, AC1999.2.1

Another artistic strategy informed the creation of the bronze *Ibis Processional Standard*, a depiction of Thoth, the Egyptian god of intelligence and writing. This object was carried by priests during ceremonial processions as the emblem, or standard, of a specific geographic region. Following the unification of Upper and Lower Egypt around 3000 B.C., the country was divided into forty-two administrative districts (nomes), each signified by regional deities and their insignia. The ibis served as the standard for an eastern Delta nome surrounding the town of Hermopolis, which was the main cult center of Thoth. The artist chose to represent the three-dimensional figure of the ibis by this flattened form, opting for a strong graphic image, thus enhancing the object's legibility as a processional standard. Nome standards are shown on a wide range of Egyptian objects. They first appear on pre-dynastic stone palettes and are later found on royal statuary and in religious scenes from tombs and temples. The sureness of its outline, the subtle contouring of its body, and the exquisite attention to detail mark the *Ibis Processional Standard* as the work of a highly accomplished artist.

Ibis Processional Standard, Egypt, Late period, 26th Dynasty, 664–525 B.C., bronze, 15 x 11 1/4 x 5/8 in. (38.1 x 28.6 x 1.6 cm), Art Museum Council Fund, M.91.73

Beaker with a Theatrical Scene

Roman Empire, probably Egypt or
Syria-Palestine, 50–100

Free-blown, painted, and gilt glass

H. 5 $\frac{5}{8}$ in. (14.3 cm); rim diam. 3 $\frac{1}{2}$ in.
(8.9 cm)

Gift of Hans Cohn

M.87.113

THIS RARE PAINTED GLASS VESSEL is the
only known example of a theatrical scene
depicted in classical art. Four actors from a
play of the Attic New Comedy—a man and
a woman, apparently in a drunken state,
accompanied by a slave and a servant boy—
look expectantly at a closed door. The
fragmentary inscription may have originally
included about 150 Greek letters. It appears
to refer to a scene involving drinking and erotic
adventures. Although the specific play or sketch is unknown, the subject
is comparable to other Roman burlesques that imitate or borrow themes
commonly found in Greek comedic theater. It has been suggested that a
scene from Meander's lost comedies might have served as inspiration.

Blown from an almost colorless, transparent glass, the flat-based beaker
has since weathered to a cloudy transparency. Restorations include about
one-fifth of the vessel, including the base, nearly all of the rim, and portions
of the body. A group of Roman painted vessels, believed to be of Egyptian
manufacture, were found in the cache of a local chieftain at Bégram in
Afghanistan. Painted glass was also produced in Syria-Palestine, which
must be considered as a second likely source.

The Hope Athena

Roman Empire, Ostia, 100–200, after a Greek original

of the late 5th century B.C., school of Pheidias

Marble

H. 86 in. (218.4 cm)

William Randolph Hearst Collection, formerly Hope Collection

51.18.12

THIS FIGURE OF ATHENA WAS EXCAVATED in Ostia, the port of Rome, in 1797, along with the museum's statue of Hygieia, goddess of health. Both once stood in large niches in the walls of a palace constructed during the Antonine period (138–161). Their size and commanding presence also

indicate that they were intended to be viewed within an impressive architectural setting.

The sculptures were acquired by Thomas Hope (1769–1831), British architect, designer, and collector of antiquities, who saw in the Athena the reflection of the great chryselephantine (gold and ivory) cult statue made for the Parthenon by Pheidias, the renowned fifth-century Greek sculptor. The Athena is possibly the work of one of Pheidias's students. This later Athena—the so-called Hope-Farnese type after the Hope statue and the other fairly complete replica in Naples—is reproduced in many Roman copies and is considered to be one of the most beautiful representations of the goddess.

This Athena originally held a spear in her left hand, and in her right, a Nike, the winged personification of victory. Extensive restorations, ordered by Thomas Hope after his acquisition of the work in 1804, included replacement of the Athena's missing arms and emblems. These additions were removed in the 1920s, and during the past decade, conservation treatments have attempted to return the Athena to the condition as excavated.

Stained Glass Panel with Angel

The Protais Master of Sées

(France, active in Normandy,

c. 1260–85)

Made in Lower Normandy, France,

c. 1270–85

Glass and metal

Diam. 32 in. (81.3 cm)

William Randolph Hearst Collection

45.21.12a

PRODUCED AT THE ZENITH

of stained glass–making in France, this panel shows the brilliant coloring and expressive design characteristic of the famous glass at the cathedrals of Chartres and Le Mans. An angel is dramatically posed within the confines of the trefoil format. Its vigorous sense of movement is conveyed through the swooping action and the erratic line of the censer chain, while its powerful image is enhanced by the highly saturated coloring of the glass.

Along with its companion panel at the museum, this angel was originally set into stone trefoil-shaped tracery high up in the central window of the axial chapel of Sées Cathedral, Normandy. Both panels flanked the main quatrefoil window showing the Virgin and Child enthroned. Following the restoration of the cathedral in the late nineteenth century, each of the panels was converted into a circular format by adding spandrels of grisaille glass.

Rosso Fiorentino [Giovanni Battista di Jacopo]

(Italy, Florence, 1494–1540)

Virgin and Child with Saints John the Baptist and Elizabeth and Two Angels, c. 1521

Oil on panel

63 1/2 x 47 in. (161.3 x 119.4 cm)

Gift of Dr. and Mrs. Herbert T. Kalmus

54.6

THIS IS ONE OF A HANDFUL of paintings by Rosso in American collections. A puzzling composition, only its attribution has not been put to question (although the painting was years ago attributed to Michelangelo). The picture can be understood only as a large-scale sketch or *ébauche* that is missing crucial elements. The exaggerated features of the figures (which could have been made less disturbing had Rosso completed the painting) prevented some critics from recognizing in them the traditional protagonists of an often-represented grouping of saints around the figures of Mary and the Christ child.

Rosso may have been aware of a composition of the same subject by Andrea del Sarto (before 1516, Louvre), from which he appears to have derived both his own composition and individual characteristics for his figures. The panel belongs to an early phase of his career, when he and other artists were formulating the unconventional style derived from Michelangelo known as Mannerism.

MAIOLICA

Renaissance art includes a wide range of decorative arts, including stained glass, Limoges enamels, Palissyware, silver, *kunstkammer* works of art, and maiolica (tin-glazed earthenware), which constitutes the most significant part of the museum's collection. Produced in Italy since the twelfth century, maiolica was raised to a significant art form during the Renaissance. The museum is particularly rich in the lustered dishes from Deruta dating from around 1500 to 1520, wares that are boldly painted with large patterned borders and with scenes, armorials, and mottoes or initials relating to the original owner. Most of these pieces are large dishes known as *piatti di pompa*, which were originally intended for display on the wall. Indeed, decoration rather than function seems to be the intention for most of these maiolica tablewares, and this is also true of the other main part of the collection, the *istoriato*, or narrative, wares from Urbino. Again mostly dishes, these pictorial wares represent a high point in Italian Renaissance ceramic art. The artists employed a brilliant palette of colors, skillfully painting rim to rim with scenes taken from classical mythology, modern popular legends, and the Bible. These *istoriato* wares often include the signature of their painters, and the museum has several fine examples by Francesco Xanto Avelli da Rovigo, one of the foremost artists working in Urbino.

Plate from the Pucci Service with Palinurus Falling Overboard, Francesco Xanto Avelli da Rovigo (Italy, Urbino, active 1528–45), made in Urbino, 1532, tin-glazed earthenware, diam. 11 3/8 in. (28.9 cm), William Randolph Hearst Collection, 50.9.28

Dish with a Young Woman, made in
Deruta, c. 1500–1530, tin-glazed
earthenware, diam. 16 1/4 in. (41.3 cm),
William Randolph Hearst Collection,
50.9.8

*Dish with Scene from Ariosto's "Orlando
Furioso,"* Francesco Xanto Avelli da
Rovigo (Italy, Urbino, active 1528–45),
made in Urbino, 1531, tin-glazed
earthenware, diam. 17 3/4 in. (45.1 cm),
William Randolph Hearst Collection,
49.26.3

Dalmatic

Holland, c. 1570

Colored wools and silk in interlocking tapestry weave

Cb. 43 1/4 in. (109.9 cm)

Gift of Mrs. Ellie Stern, Bullocks Wilshire, the Costume Council, and Mrs. Madeline B. Nelson

M.79.117

THIS DALMATIC IS PART OF A RARE complete set of ecclesiastical vestments surviving the troubled period of the Reformation in sixteenth-century Holland. The set can be dated to 1570 from an inscription woven in the banderoles on one of its companion pieces at the Metropolitan Museum of Art. The motto translates: "We are bent, not broken by the waves," a particularly appropriate sentiment for Dutch Catholics. From the 1560s they had endured Protestant hostility against the Church and its clergy, a situation that prevailed in Utrecht until 1580, when Roman Catholic public worship was suppressed.

The dalmatic bears the coats of arms of the van der Geer and van

Culenborch families of Utrecht, indicating that the set was probably commissioned for use in a private chapel, a timely decision in light of events. The biblical imagery is also fitting; the bull rushes rising above the waves allude both to the inscription and to Moses, who led the Israelites out of their bondage in Egypt.

The message of salvation has been interpreted with virtuosity. The dalmatic is woven in colored wools in a flat tapestry weave, a technique used extensively in the Low Countries but usually for large "picture" tapestry wall hangings. Combining this technique with embroidery, the weaver has created an illusion of pile velvet on the richly textured surface.

One of a Pair of Tazzas

Jean Dolahaye (France, active 1579–1611) and
Nicolas de Villiers II (France, active 1582–1613)
Made in Paris, 1583–84 and later
Silver gilt
Diam. 11 ¹⁄₂ in. (29.2 cm)
Gift of Selim K. Zilkha
M.91.347.2

PARISIAN SILVER OF THE SIXTEENTH CENTURY is extremely uncommon, most having been lost due to wars and changes in fashion. The only other known examples made by Jean Delahaye and Nicolas de Villiers II are in the Vatican collection. This highly decorated silver was intended for display on the sideboard or buffet on grand ceremonial occasions rather than for use and was probably part of a larger service.

This tazza from the museum's pair is chased with a scene after engravings by Philips Galle (1537–1612), which in turn were derived from hunting tapestries designed by Jan van der Straet (1523–1605) for the Medici in Florence in the 1560s. The scene is emblematic of one of the four major continents, suggesting that the museum's tazzas were originally part of a set of four. On this example, Europe is represented by a game hunt in a forest landscape. It is likely that this pair survived because it was exported in the mid-seventeenth century to England, where silver tended to be handed down in family collections rather than being refashioned according to the prevailing style.

Ugo da Carpi (Italy, active in Venice, Rome, and Bologna,
active c. 1502–32)
Diogenes (after Parmigianino), c. 1527
Chiaroscuro woodcut from 4 blocks
$19\,^1/_{16}$ x $13\,^{11}/_{16}$ in. (48.4 x 34.8 cm)
Gift of Philippa Calnan in memory of her mother Matilda Loeser Calnan
M.2001.176

UGO DA CARPI'S *DIOGENES* is the artist's masterpiece, a tour de force of the medium of chiaroscuro woodcut, a form of printing that uses multiple wood blocks to create the effect of a wash drawing. *Diogenes* is based on a drawing provided by Ugo's contemporary Francesco Parmigianino, whose name appears along with Ugo's on the book in the lower left corner—clear testament of the work's collaborative nature. Ugo's use of broad areas of color and subtly defined tones reflects his direct experience of Raphael and his workshop in Rome after Ugo moved there in 1517. The figure of Diogenes, with its bold foreshortening and complex pose, reveals the unmistakable influence of Michelangelo's Sistine Chapel frescoes.

The museum's impression of the print is an early one made from four blocks: a key block in black ink, defining the image's outlines, and three tone blocks in different shades of green. Ugo claimed to have invented the technique of chiaroscuro woodcut, although this was a false boast; he was, however, the first to sign his blocks and among the first to copyright his designs. There are only fourteen documented prints by the artist, although many others have been attributed to him.

The ancient Greek philosopher Diogenes taught that the virtuous life is the simple life. He discarded conventional comforts and chose to live in a barrel (visible in the background of Ugo's print). The plucked chicken is a reference to Aristotle's description of man as a "featherless biped."

Rembrandt Harmensz van Rijn (Holland, 1606–1669)

The Raising of Lazarus, c. 1630

Oil on panel

37 $^{15}/_{16}$ x 32 in. (96.4 x 81.3 cm)

Gift of H. F. Ahmanson and Company in memory of Howard F. Ahmanson

M.72.67.2

THE RAISING OF LAZARUS BELONGS to Rembrandt's early years in Leiden, his native city, where he set up a studio after having briefly studied in Amsterdam under Pieter Lastman. The strong contrasts of dark and light areas and the expressiveness of the composition can certainly be attributed to the distant influence of Caravaggio, made available to Rembrandt through the works of the Utrecht painters who had brought back to Holland the innovations and spirit of the Italian master. Rembrandt, however, does not focus the strongest light on the biblical story's main protagonists, Christ and Lazarus, whom he keeps in half-shadows, but shines it instead on the face of Mary Magdalene, thus shifting the narrative to the witnesses of the scene and by extension to the viewers of the picture.

Rembrandt often altered the character, if not the very essence, of biblical representations by introducing innovations whose strength lies in their subtlety. For instance, he sets the story, usually represented in broad daylight, in a somber cave or catacomb. Likewise, he replaces the image of a triumphant and confident Christ with that of a miracle worker whose expression betrays amazement at his own deeds and power. It is not known for whom Rembrandt may have painted this work, which even so early in his career shows distinctive originality.

Georges de La Tour (France, 1593–1652)
The Magdalen with the Smoking Flame, c. 1638–40
Oil on canvas
46 1/16 x 36 1/8 in. (117 x 91.8 cm)
Gift of The Ahmanson Foundation
M.77.73

A NATIVE OF LORRAINE, a province with a significant school of painting, Georges de La Tour remains a mysterious, almost mythical, figure. He never left his native province, yet the sophistication of his paintings, which found favor with the most discerning collectors, is indisputable. Their stark compositions and realism, as well as the artist's representation of artificial sources of light, betray a link to Caravaggio that can be explained by La Tour's familiarity with the work of Jean Le Clerc, himself a follower of the Italian master.

La Tour painted the subject of the Magdalen on several occasions. Two paintings, respectively in New York and Washington, D.C., are particularly close in size and composition to the museum's picture, yet the starkness and austere purity of the Los Angeles Magdalen is exceptional. La Tour's compositions achieve their power through a reduction of narrative effects. Here, while the objects—each one carefully detailed—situate the image in the broader context of a *vanitas* picture—a well-established genre at the time of the Counter-Reformation—the focus is in the meditative gaze of the Magdalen. Although La Tour set the impressive skull in the center of his composition, he elevates to the upper tier of the canvas his true subject: the glowing space around the smoking flame, symbolic in the words of Saint John of the Cross of "the living flame of love."

Michiel Sweerts (Flanders, 1618–1664, active in Italy)

Plague in an Ancient City, c. 1653(?)

Oil on canvas

$46^{3}/_{4}$ x $67^{1}/_{4}$ in. (118.7 x 170.8 cm)

Gift of The Ahmanson Foundation

AC1997.10.1

MICHIEL SWEERTS, A FLEMISH ARTIST active in Rome, became known
as a painter of genre scenes—a specialty among Northern painters in
Italy—and of particularly arresting portraits. Nothing in his oeuvre, however,
prefigured the scale and metaphysical depth of this painting, his undisputed
masterpiece. Although a realistic description of illness and death, the
painting is also an allegory of human fate and salvation. Death, decay, and
sorrow occupy the fore- and middle ground of the composition. In the
center of the picture, a standing man, sometimes identified as a
philosopher, is flanked by a seminude female figure—perhaps an allegory.
His gesture is relayed by an ancient priest on the steps of a temple, inviting

the viewer to direct his or her attention to the shrine. The picture contrasts life and death, darkness and light, despair and redemption.

Renaissance and Baroque artists who lived through plague epidemics were occasionally commissioned to paint commemorative pictures or ex-votos, drawing their inspiration from biblical stories or the writings of ancient historians. Sweerts's *Plague* appears to have been painted shortly after an epidemic that decimated Rome in 1648, yet the circumstances of its commission are not known today.

Sweerts was a profoundly devout and somewhat tormented man who may have experienced a religious crisis around the time he painted this work. Shortly afterward he left Rome, eventually joining a group of French missionaries bound for the East, and died in unknown circumstances in Goa, India. It has been argued that this singular painting may have indicated a new, classical departure for Sweerts. It also illustrates how sensitive he was to the metaphysical currents of his time.

Carlo Maratta (Italy, Rome, 1625–1713)
Study for an Allegorical Figure of Africa, c. 1674–77
Red chalk on paper, laid down
17 x 12³⁄₈ in. (43.2 x 31.4 cm)
Purchased in memory of Lorser Feitelson with funds provided by the Graphic Arts Council,
Dart Industries, Inc., and Ticor Corporations
M.79.10

CARLO MARATTA WAS ONE OF THE MOST ACTIVE and influential artists of seventeenth-century Italy, and one of the finest draftsmen of his age. In contrast to many of his Baroque contemporaries, his art was devoted to a classical clarity and simplicity that had originated two hundred years earlier with Raphael.

In 1674 Maratta was commissioned to fresco the audience hall of the Palazzo Altieri, the Roman family home of Pope Clement X. The central section of the vault was devoted to *An Allegory of Clemency* (an allusion to the pope's name), and Maratta planned to fill the rest of the ceiling with allegorical personifications of Christian virtues and representations of the

four parts of the known world (Europe, America, Africa, and Asia). Only *An Allegory of Clemency* was completed. The rest of Maratta's decorative scheme is known only through preparatory drawings, such as this bold and powerful red-chalk study.

Somewhat whimsically, the allegorical figure of Africa wears an elephant's head as a helmet, while a lion, a crocodile, and a snake (all associated with the then barely explored continent) accompany her. Maratta's sense of humor extends to the putto kneeling in the foreground, who gestures in alarm at the approaching snake. The four continents were meant to be painted in the ceiling's spandrels, thus the drawing's unusual shape.

FRENCH OIL SKETCHES

Oil sketch is a generic term used to describe paintings, usually intimate in scale, that represent various moments of an artist's creative process. Some may be first thoughts for large compositions, wall-size paintings, or frescoes; others are fragmentary studies for details of larger works. Another category

Simon Vouet (France, 1590–1649), *Model for Altarpiece in Saint Peter's*, 1625, oil on canvas, 16 x 24 $^1/_4$ in. (40.6 x 61.6 cm), The Ciechanowiecki Collection, gift of The Ahmanson Foundation, M.2000.179.2

is landscape studies, executed from nature long before the Impressionists made this approach to painting a trademark. Unfinished paintings, or *ébauches*, are yet another variety of oil sketches.

Although artists often painted studies for later compositions, oil studies were usually not intended for public display or private collection. Starting in the eighteenth century, however, partially under the influence of Flemish or Venetian artists who had achieved fame for handling paint with spirited freedom, artists devoted more attention to oil sketches, or in some cases, painted in a free manner that obliterated the artificial division between the styles of the study and of the finished work. Likewise, collectors began acquiring sketches, not only as documents, but also for their aesthetic quality.

Baron François Gérard (Italy, Rome, 1770–1837, active in France), *The 10th of August, 1792*, 1794, oil on canvas, 42 x 56³/₄ in. (106.7 x 144.1 cm), The Ciechanowiecki Collection, gift of The Ahmanson Foundation, M.2000.179.36

The museum's collection of oil sketches includes works ranging from seventeenth-century artists Simon Vouet and Louis de La Hyre to the nineteenth century's Théodore Rousseau, Jean-Baptiste Carpeaux, and Félix Ziem, with a particularly impressive representation of Neoclassical artists, such as Baron Gérard, whose unfinished *The 10th of August, 1792* is especially noteworthy.

François Boucher (France, 1703–1770), *Project for a Cartouche: An Allegory of Minerva, Fame, History, and Faith Overcoming Ignorance and Time*, c. 1727, oil on canvas, 20¹/₄ x 24¹/₂ in. (51.4 x 62.2 cm), purchased with funds provided anonymously in memory of Dr. Charles Henry Strub by exchange, AC1998.148.1

Bed Hanging with Pegasus and the Nine Muses

Italy, c. 1700

Silk and metallic thread embroidery on plain-weave silk ground

134 1/2 x 131 in. (341.6 x 332.7 cm)

Purchased with funds provided by the Costume Council, Richard and Lenore Wayne, the Costume
and Textiles Department, Inez K. Bell, Boyd and Helena Krout, Robinsons-May, Alice and Nahum
Lainer, Jacqueline and Arthur Burdorf, Mr. and Mrs. William M. Carpenter, Eva P. Elkins, Linda and
Jim Freund, Nelly and Jim Kilroy, Maggie Pexton Murray, Terry and Dennis Stanfill, Mr. and Mrs.
David Sydorick, Mrs. Carl W. Barrow, Genevieve W. and Marvin M. Chesebro, Dorothy Cutler, Mrs.
Ernest M. Lever, and Mr. and Mrs. H. Grant Theis

AC1998.248.1

UNTIL THE END OF THE EIGHTEENTH CENTURY, beds were the most important piece of household furniture, and textiles were their most valuable component. In wealthy households, the main bedroom, which also served as a reception room, and its decorative program reflected the family's status. Possibly a wedding gift, the museum's hanging was part of an elaborate set of bed furnishings.

References to the ideal aristocratic pursuits of poetry and the arts appear on the hanging. At the top, the winged horse Pegasus strikes Mount Helicon, causing the Hippocrene spring of poetic inspiration to flow. Mount Helicon is the home of the nine Muses, who are arrayed around the hanging in individual landscapes. The figures are surrounded by an exotic and sometimes fanciful assortment of fountains, plants, animals, birds, and insects. Sources for these images included Renaissance interpretations of Roman domestic wall decoration and printed emblem books. Emblems, allegorical designs expressing an abstract thought in visual form, are closely related to poetry. Although the late sixteenth century marked the height of interest in emblems, they remained part of an aristocrat's education well into the eighteenth century.

A masterpiece of the embroiderer's art, this hanging was the product of professional workshops. The delicate shading used to render flesh tones and the subtle handling of volume could be achieved only by a highly experienced needleworker.

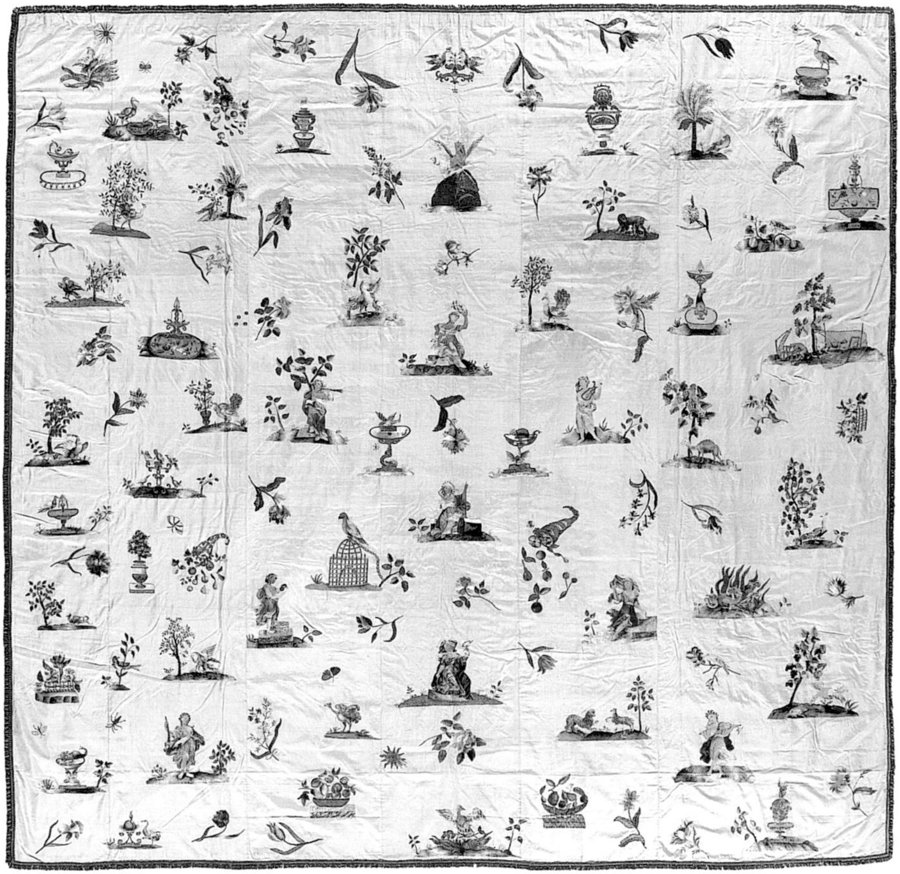

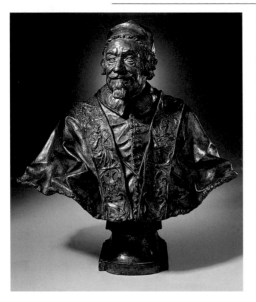

Domenico Guidi (Italy, Rome, 1628–1701)

Portrait of Pope Alexander VIII, 1690

Gilded terracotta on gilded wood socle

36 1/4 (including socle) x 32 1/2 x 17 1/2 in.

(92.1 x 82.6 x 44.5 cm)

Purchased with funds provided by the William Randolph Hearst Foundation

47.8.30

THIS GRANDIOSE, GILDED TERRACOTTA portrait of Pope Alexander VIII (1610–1691, elected pope in 1689) was commissioned by his great-nephew, Cardinal Pietro Ottoboni, a brilliant patron of the arts. Domenico Guidi's artistry is displayed in the commanding turn of the pope's head; in the vigorous modeling of the details of the stole, which depict Saints Peter and Paul and the Ottoboni coat of arms; and in the energetic verve of the fur-lined edge of the cape (*mozzetta*), with its strong, syncopated curves and angles.

Guidi's talent has only recently become better recognized. He was long overshadowed in art history by the brilliance of Gianlorenzo Bernini, for whom he carved marble, and Alessandro Algardi, for whom he cast bronzes. Indeed, Guidi was one of the few sculptors in Rome who was capable of casting his own compositions in bronze without recourse to a foundry specialist.

Benedetto Luti (Italy, Rome, 1666–1724)

Head of an Apostle, 1712

Pastel on paper

16 1/8 x 13 in. (41 x 33 cm)

Gift of the 1996 Collectors Committee

AC1996.29.1

BENEDETTO LUTI ABSORBED, while at the same time softened, the great Roman classical tradition in painting as exemplified by artists from Raphael to Carlo Maratta, Luti's immediate predecessor. He was also one of the great colorists of his age, a skill he put to admirable use in the many pastel and colored-chalk drawings for which he is justly famous.

The masterful *Head of an Apostle* is from a set of twelve pastel drawings of the apostles. Which one of the twelve Luti intended is unclear because he omitted the traditional attributes associated with each (although, given the presence of an open book, it is certainly one of the four evangelists: Matthew, Mark, Luke, or John). These portraits are thus closer to character studies than they are to religious images. The museum's drawing is the most vigorous and dramatic of the group, notable especially for Luti's virtuoso handling of the chalks and for the extraordinary effect of soft and shimmering tactility in the rendering of the apostle's beard.

Luti animated his subject by turning the apostle's head abruptly to the right, as if suddenly called away from the book open before him. Deep in

thought, his faced bathed in (divine?) light, the apostle is granted a degree of psychological and physical intensity appropriate to the Lord's representative. The immediacy, fluency, and grace of Luti's pastels owe a debt to the sixteenth-century master Correggio, whose art enjoyed a great revival in the eighteenth century.

Jean-Antoine Watteau

(France, 1684–1721)

The Perfect Accord, 1719

Oil on panel

13 x 11 in. (33 x 28 cm)

Gift of The Ahmanson Foundation

AC1999.18.1

JEAN-ANTOINE WATTEAU invented and perfected the *fête galante*, a genre of compositions showing full-length figures, albeit in small scale, engaged in activities—conversation, music playing, promenading, merrymaking—that can best be described as the pursuit of happiness. The genre flourished also in the works of his followers, Nicolas Lancret and Jean-Baptiste Pater. Watteau never explained the meaning of his compositions, which were given titles by others and are as seductive as their interpretations remain mysterious. *The Perfect Accord* is one such elusive masterpiece. An ugly old man plays a flute, accompanying a young and beautiful singer, while a third figure, seen from the back and garbed in a theatrical costume, plays the guitar. Behind them, a couple walks by. A statue of Pan on the right contributes to setting the bucolic and mildly erotic tone of the scene.

Watteau prepared his compositions with numerous drawings (a study for the flute player is at the J. Paul Getty Museum) but did not attempt to ensure his works a lasting life. He reused panels, scraping off or roughly covering former compositions. This panel was originally part of a coach door on which Watteau had painted its owner's coat of arms. It was later returned to Watteau, who cut it in half and used one half to paint *The Italian Serenade*, now in Stockholm, and the other to paint first a composition with several figures (both the coat of arms and this composition are visible in X rays) and finally *The Perfect Accord*.

The Great Lamentation

Originally modeled by Massimiliano Soldani-Benzi (Italy, Florence, 1656–1740), c. 1715

Made at the Ginori Porcelain Manufactory, Doccia, c. 1745

Porcelain

26 $\frac{1}{2}$ x 25 x 23 $\frac{1}{2}$ in. (67.3 x 63.5 x 59.7 cm)

Purchased with funds provided by Neal Castleman and Ellen Hoffman-Castleman by exchange, The Ahmanson Foundation, Antonio Mariani of Antonio's Antiques by exchange, Peter Norton, Bob Looker, Frank Baxter, Camilla Chandler Frost, Eli Broad, Lynda Resnick, the Iris and B. Gerald Cantor Foundation, Julian Ganz, Yvonne Lenart, Dan Belin in honor of Wally Weisman, Sandy Terner, John Hotchkis, Judith Gaillard Jones, Chris Walker, Mrs. James Porter Fiske by exchange, and Willard G. Clark

M.2001.78a–b

MASSIMILIANO SOLDANI-BENZI was one of the two greatest Florentine Baroque sculptors. When he was only twenty two years old, he was sent by the Grand Duke Cosimo de'Medici to perfect his training in Rome and Paris. Soldani-Benzi was head of the Florentine mint for forty years and during that time designed a quantity of medals, decorative objects, freestanding sculptures, and reliefs. *The Great Lamentation* (also called *Large Pietà* to distinguish it from his less elaborate Pietà) was unparalleled in his oeuvre for its complexity and size.

After Soldani-Benzi's death, his son sold his wax models to the Marchese Carlo Ginori, who had established a porcelain manufactory in 1737 at the town of Doccia, near Florence. Since the Renaissance, the princely courts of Europe had tried to reproduce the fine porcelain of China without true success until the manufactory at Meissen achieved its aims in 1710. The manufactory at Vienna soon followed; it was probably Vienna that inspired Ginori to establish his. A true figure of the Enlightenment, Ginori was appointed ambassador by the Tuscan senate when control of Tuscany was transferred to the Habsburgs in Vienna. There he secured the services of the porcelain painter Karl Anreiter von Zirnfeld, who returned with him to Doccia.

Spectacularly colored in the vivid palette preferred by Anreiter, *The Great Lamentation* is a tour de force of porcelain sculpture. The Ginori manufactory produced only three porcelain examples of this ambitious

composition. The others are in the Corsini collection (Florence) and the
Nationalmuseum (Stockholm). The museum's example, believed to be the
one painted by Anreiter and taken back with him to Vienna when his
contract with Ginori expired, was purchased from the Hispanic Society.

POLYCHROMED SCULPTURE

Circle of Domenico Antonio Vaccaro (Italy, Naples, 1680–1750), *Saint Michael Casting Satan into Hell*, c. 1725, polychromed wood with glass, 51 $1/2$ x 27 $1/4$ x 24 $3/4$ in. (130.8 x 69.2 x 62.9 cm), gift of The Ahmanson Foundation, M.82.7

The museum's renowned collection of sculptures that are painted, or polychromed, heightens the visitor's senses to the interaction of form and color. The museum's polychromed sculptures range from the austere *Deposition from the Cross* (circle of Daniel Mauch, c. 1515) to the fanciful but dramatic *Saint Michael Casting Satan into Hell* (c. 1725), whose subject comes from the Book of Revelation (12:7–10). The archangel Michael battles the "dragon," Satan, and casts him out of heaven. In the museum's sculpture, Saint Michael's triumphant, delicate beauty contrasts with Satan's ferocity. The wonderful patterns and colors of Saint Michael's wings and costume are enhanced by the ruby-colored glass in his sandals and armor; both figures have glass eyes.

The grand and gracefully proportioned *Archangel Raphael* (c. 1600), nearly six feet tall, was once accompanied by a small figure of Tobias, lost before the sculpture was purchased by the museum. The subject, therefore, has also been interpreted as the Guardian Angel (Raphael's guise when he accompanies Tobias on his journeys). Either interpretation lends support to its attribution to the Neapolitan school because Raphael was one of the patron saints of Naples. Much of the figure was polychromed in the painstaking technique *sgraffito* (*estofado* in Spanish), in which most of the sculpture was covered in gold leaf and then painted. The artist incised the painted layer with a stylus, creating patterns in the brilliant metal revealed underneath.

The cruciform designs in the archangel's armor are more disciplined than those in the museum's Spanish sculptures of

Saint Mark (attributed to Alonso Berruguete, c. 1560) and the Pietà (unknown artist, c. 1725), in which the patterns are more freely sketched. The Pietà is especially remarkable because it was made almost entirely of cloth—either in the form of macerated linen fibers, rigidified yardage (*tela encolada*), or possibly a real dress (for the Virgin Mary), which was gilded and then colored with a transparent red glaze. Mary's head and hands are plaster, and her eyes are glass.

The lightness of cloth sculptures made them especially popular for religious processions in Spain. These sculptures were frequently commissioned by penitential or charitable confraternities. Some were given to churches, but others were discarded because they were considered to be nothing more than ephemeral decorations. This Pietà is the only one of its kind in an American museum.

Archangel Raphael (Italy, Naples, c. 1600), polychromed and gilded wood, h. 70 in. (177.8 cm), gift of Anna Bing Arnold, M.77.52

Pietà (Spain, Seville or Córdoba?, c. 1725), polychromed plaster, macerated linen fibers, gesso- or glue-soaked fabric, wood, glass, and other materials, 45 1/4 x 44 1/2 x 33 in. (115 x 113 x 84 cm), purchased with funds provided by Eugene V. Klein and Mary Jones Gaston in memory of her parents, Mr. and Mrs. Charles Stone Jones, by exchange, M.2000.12

Candlesticks with Apollo and Daphne

Designed by George Michael Moser (Switzerland, 1706–1783, active in England)

Made in London, c. 1745

Gilt bronze

14 $\frac{1}{4}$ x 7 x 7 in. (36.2 x 17.8 x 17.8 cm) each

Decorative Arts Council Fund in honor of Sondra Ott

M.2001.20.1a–b,2a–b

THESE ROCOCO-STYLE candlesticks are among the earliest-known examples of ormolu (gilt bronze) made in England. First developed in Paris during the late seventeenth century, ormolu was intended for lighting, furniture mounts, and clocks in the luxury interior. In England, however, the use of ormolu was relatively unknown until the 1760s and then only among a small circle of artists and patrons. The Rococo, which originated in Paris during the 1720s, was characterized by delicate sculptural forms of rock, shell, and scrollwork, and a tendency toward asymmetry. George Michael Moser probably mastered this latest fashion during his training in Geneva and Paris. When he settled in London he worked as a chaser of gold watchcases and snuffboxes in the Rococo style.

Moser's design shows the moment from Ovid's *Metamorphoses* when Daphne transforms into a laurel tree to escape the amorous clutches of the love-struck Apollo. The figure of Daphne is closely related to a design for a candlestick by Gilles-Marie Oppenord (1672–1742) of the 1730s, but Moser must have derived the Rococo scroll- and shellwork and twisting asymmetrical forms from the engraved work of the goldsmith and architect Juste-Aurèle Meissonnier (1695–1750).

François Boucher (France, 1703–1770)

Bacchus and Ariadne, 1747–66

Tapestry-woven wool and silk

141 x 216 in. (358.1 x 548.6 cm)

Gift of J. Paul Getty

52.32

BACCHUS, THE GOD OF WINE, has just arrived on the island of Naxos, where he finds Ariadne, the daughter of the king of Crete, lying on the shore. She is lamenting that her lover, Theseus, abandoned her while she slept. In François Boucher's depiction of the story, Bacchus is seen rushing up to offer comfort to the stricken young woman.

Once part of a suite of tapestries depicting nine scenes from Loves of the Gods, the museum's tapestry was woven at the Royal Beauvais Manufactory, founded in 1664. In 1736 Boucher was invited to produce drawings for tapestries; from then until his death in 1770, Beauvais produced tapestries almost exclusively from drawings by the artist—a collaboration that bolstered the fortunes of Beauvais and the success of the Rococo interior.

The suite, Loves of the Gods, and this particular scene from it were woven at Beauvais many times between 1747 and 1766 as both royal and private commissions. Since all the royal commands of the series are accounted for, the museum's tapestry must be from a private commission. The master craftsmen of Beauvais admirably captured Boucher's famous luminous flesh tones. Years of accumulated dirt, however, had almost completely obscured this aspect of the tapestry. In 1996 *Bacchus and Ariadne* was sent to England for conservation. There it was washed and lined for support. The tapestry was renewed and Boucher's genius became visible again.

Giovanni Battista Tiepolo
(Italy, Venice, 1696–1770)
A Fallen Angel, c. 1752
Red and white chalk on faded blue paper
10 1/2 x 12 1/4 in.
(26.7 x 31.1 cm)
Gift of the Graphic Arts Council
in honor of Ebria Feinblatt
M.84.21

A FALLEN ANGEL is a study for one of the figures in Giovanni Battista Tiepolo's altarpiece of 1752, *The Fall of the Rebel Angels*, made for the chapel of the Prince-Bishop's residence at Würzburg, Germany, where the artist and his studio (including his son Giovanni Domenico) created one of the most splendid decorative ensembles in European art. Boldly modeled and brilliantly lit, the figure's elongated torso (characteristic of Tiepolo's approach to anatomy) is defined by the dramatic contrast of shadow (expressed by the deftly applied red chalk) and light (suggested by a few masterful strokes of white chalk). The blue of the paper, now somewhat faded, is used as a halftone mediating between light and dark, while the figure's contour is rendered with a form-defining line, both agitated and nimble. *A Fallen Angel* exemplifies Tiepolo's draftsmanship at its highest level.

Tiepolo used his drawings, hundreds of which survive, as essential aids in the production of his oil paintings and especially for the dozens of frescoes he executed in his native Venice, throughout northern Italy, and in Germany. At the same time, many of his drawings were conceived independently of painting projects. His work is renowned for its extreme Rococo elegance, the brilliance and luminosity of its color, and its daring and dazzling spatial effects.

John Deare (England, 1759/60–1798, active in Italy)

The Judgment of Jupiter, 1786–c. 1790

Marble

58 $\frac{1}{4}$ x 117 $\frac{1}{4}$ x approx. 10 in. (148 x 297.8 x 25.4 cm)

Gift of Anna Bing Arnold

M.79.37

THIS IS THE MOST IMPORTANT Neoclassical relief in the United States, carved by a virtuoso sculptor whose life ended in less than forty years. John Deare was the youngest to win the Royal Academy's Gold Medal (1780, in sculpture); in 1785 he was awarded a stipend to go to Rome. There he immersed himself in the study of classical antiquities and sharpened his skill as a draftsman. *The Judgment of Jupiter* was carved in Rome. Deare died there, never returning to England.

The relief depicts an episode that lay at the origin of the *Iliad*. The goddess of Discord was excluded from the wedding of Peleus and Thetis. She threw a gold apple inscribed "to the fairest" among the guests, sparking a competition among the goddesses Venus, Athena, and Diana that ultimately led to the Trojan War. Here, Jupiter points to his messenger, Mercury, who flies overhead; he will deliver the apple to a shepherd named Paris, chosen by Jupiter to decide the contest in his stead.

The composition is set up in varying rhythms: the central section shows Jupiter facing the competing goddesses, with Mercury flying overhead; they are flanked on the left by Thetis and Peleus and on the right by departing warriors. The marble is chiseled so that the relief varies from near-freestanding figures to almost complete flatness, as though engraved like an antique cameo. Several figures were directly inspired by ancient Roman statues. In all, this masterpiece embodies the cold purity, beauty, and perfection that are the quintessential characteristics of Neoclassical art.

Jean-Auguste-Dominique Ingres

(France, 1780–1867)

Portrait of Thomas Church, 1816

Graphite on paper

7 15/16 x 6 1/4 in. (20.2 x 15.9 cm)

Purchased with funds provided by the Loula D. Lasker Bequest and Museum Associates Acquisition Fund

M.67.62

THOMAS CHURCH (1758–1821) was a fifty-eight-year-old English surgeon visiting Rome on the Grand Tour when Jean-Auguste-Dominique Ingres drew his portrait. The artist, who had been studying and working in Rome since 1806, supported himself at the time by making portrait drawings of foreign sitters. In *Portrait of Thomas Church*, Ingres used a finely sharpened pencil to capture the sitter's face and personality, while broader and more loosely applied strokes were used for the rest of the figure. The contrast between the highly finished head and the more impressionistically rendered torso is characteristic of the artist's style, and it provides a tension between the apparent spontaneity of a frozen moment and the timelessness expressed by Church's impassive face.

The essence of art resided in draftsmanship, according to Ingres, who worshiped Raphael and considered himself heir to the classical tradition. The sureness of his touch, his free and sinuous yet exacting line (capable of suggesting the sheen of silk or the roughness of wool), make his portrait drawings among the most sublime expressions of the power of linear definition. *Portrait of Thomas Church* was produced at the height of Ingres's powers and is one of his finest and freshest character studies. Ingres also drew a pendant portrait of Church's younger brother, Joseph, now in the Virginia Museum of Fine Arts.

Toilet Mirror

Designed by Philip Webb (England, 1831–1915) and (side and door panels) by Edward Burne-Jones (England, 1833–1898)

Made by Morris, Marshall, Faulkner and Co., London, 1862

Walnut, gesso, paint, gilding, glass, and brass

33 x 29 x 8 $1/4$ in. (83.8 x 73.7 x 21 cm)

Purchased with funds provided by Mr. and Mrs. Russell McKinnon, William Randolph Hearst Collection, Walter Stein, J. Paul Getty, Mr. and Mrs. Danny Kaye, Anna Popper, Colonel and Mrs. George J. Denis, Mr. and Mrs. Arthur Hornblower, Jr., and Mary B. Reagan Bequest M.2001.19.1

THE BRITISH ARTS AND CRAFTS movement extolled handmade, vernacular-inspired furnishings over industrial, classically derived ones. Of all the movement's protagonists, William Morris (1834–1896) had the most far-reaching influence. In 1861 he established the firm of Morris, Marshall, Faulkner and Company to protest and provide an alternative to the manufacture of "soulless" factory goods. (The firm was reorganized as Morris and Company in 1875.) This toilet mirror is an early product of the firm, whose goals included raising the status of the decorative arts to equal that of fine arts and architecture. Among the firm's associates was the Pre-Raphaelite painter Edward Burne-Jones, who designed the figures on the mirror, and the architect Philip Webb, who conceived its form.

Webb designed this piece in the first year of the firm's existence for his friend Warington Taylor, who became the company's business manager in 1865. Like other supporters of the Arts and Crafts movement, Taylor embraced traditional English arts, which were considered purer and more "moral" than imported styles. In accordance with these principles, Webb designed the mirror in a startlingly simple form, influenced by English vernacular furniture. And while the highly decorated figures would seem in opposition to the form, they are not, since they are in the Gothic style favored by early Arts and Crafts reformers.

Edgar Degas (France, 1834–1917)
Giovanna and Giuliana Bellelli, 1865–66
Oil on canvas
36 1/4 x 28 3/4 in. (92.1 x 73 cm)
Mr. and Mrs. George Gard De Sylva Collection
M.46.3.3

THE SITTERS, GIOVANNA AND GIULIANA BELLELLI, were Degas's cousins, the daughters of his aunt Laura Bellelli and her husband, Gennaro Bellelli. Degas visited his relatives in Florence on several occasions, most importantly in 1858 and 1859, at which time he conceived the large portrait of the family now at the Musée d'Orsay, Paris. Numerous studies and independent portraits relate to the large composition. Like the famous Bellelli family portrait, the museum's portrait conveys the physical, and by implication, psychological distance between the sitters.

It is possible that working in Paris on this double portrait of relatives in Italy, Degas relied not only on sketches but also on photographs, as

suggested by a drawing for the composition in the Museum Boijmans Van Beuningen, Rotterdam. In it, the careful delineation of the figures—so different from Degas's spirited draftsmanship—may indeed betray the painter's attention to a photographic model. If that was the case, the daguerreotype would have been for Degas but an aide-mémoire: His painting eschews the stiffness and trite presentation of contemporary studio photography.

The painting's degree of completion has also been the subject of some speculation. Although it is often dated 1862–64, recent scholarship has convincingly argued that its proper date is 1865–66. By then, Degas could certainly have adopted a more cursive style, leaving areas of his compositions almost unfinished.

Adolph Menzel (Germany, 1815–1905)

Studies for "The Broken Jug" by Heinrich von Kleist, 1876

Graphite on paper

9³/₄ x 14⁷/₈ in. (24.8 x 37.8 cm)

Gift of the 2001 Collectors Committee

M.2001.61.1

ADOLPH MENZEL WAS THE MOST PROMINENT artist in Germany from
the 1850s until his death in 1905 and ranks with Edgar Degas as one of
the greatest draftsmen of the nineteenth century. Painter, illustrator, teacher,
and tireless chronicler of life in Berlin, Menzel led the way both to Realism
and to Impressionism. His motto was "not a day without drawing," and he
followed his advice with unflagging diligence, producing more than ten
thousand drawings.

   Studies for "The Broken Jug" is a preparatory drawing for one of
Menzel's engraved illustrations commissioned for an anniversary edition of
Heinrich von Kleist's comic play *The Broken Jug* (1808). A landmark of
German Romantic theater, the play is set in an early-eighteenth-century
Dutch village where the central character, Judge Adam, finds himself
presiding over a case in which he is himself the culprit. In the opening
scene, Adam examines in a mirror the head wound he received the
previous night while attempting to seduce the village girl Eve. At the same
time he nurses his leg, injured while leaping from Eve's window. In the

upper right corner, Menzel inserted a masterfully rendered close-up view of this leg.

With virtuoso control of his preferred drawing instrument—the carpenter's pencil—the artist articulated the outlines of his figures with the pencil's sharp point, while with its flat side he evoked the fall of fabric over solid form through broad parallel strokes. An ambidextrous draftsman, Menzel executed *Studies for "The Broken Jug"* with his left hand.

Paul Cézanne (France, 1839–1906)

Forest, c. 1894

Oil on canvas

45 3/4 x 32 in. (116.2 x 81.3 cm)

Wallis Foundation Fund in memory of Hal B. Wallis

AC1992.161.1

FOREST IS AN EXUBERANT CANVAS in which Paul Cézanne abandons his usual restraint, economy of means, and strict sense of composition in favor of jubilant colors and improvisation. The red tones of the earth, luminous patches of blue sky, and luxuriant vegetation indicate the painting was executed in the artist's native Provence, which Cézanne evokes with accuracy.

In this painting Cézanne develops a motif familiar in his work since the 1870s: the depiction of trees or thickets seen up close. Cézanne's dense and powerful compositions acknowledge a debt to the late landscapes of Courbet, and to Pissarro, in whose company Cézanne had worked earlier in his career. In *Forest*, one of his most audacious compositions, Cézanne takes even further the innovations of these painters by eliminating a human presence or precise topography. The modernity and originality of such compositions did not escape the attention of critics and artists, in particular the younger artists associated with the Pont-Aven School, who recognized the liberating force implied in the radicalism of Cézanne's paintings and saw in them a model for their own aesthetic quest.

Auguste Rodin (France, 1840–1917)
Severed Head of Saint John the Baptist, c. 1887–1907
Marble
8 x 15³⁄₄ x 13¹⁄₂ in. (20.3 x 40 x 34.3 cm)
Museum purchase made possible by the Iris and B. Gerald Cantor Foundation in memory of B. Gerald Cantor
AC1998.139.1

THE GOSPEL OF ST. MATTHEW (14:7–11) recounts Saint John the Baptist's decapitation at the order of King Herod. This episode from the New Testament became a preferred subject of the late-nineteenth-century artistic movement Symbolism. To Rodin this sculpture represented the Belgian nation's martyrdom in World War I. Rodin cherished Belgium because he had spent some of the happiest years of his life there early in his career. The sculpture was inscribed to the queen of Belgium as a personal gift in 1916, and Rodin had it consigned to the care of the

American dancer Loïe Fuller, one of his greatest promoters. Because of the chaotic conditions of the war and Rodin's death in 1917, the sculpture was not delivered to its rightful owner until 1926. The queen's son Leopold III inherited and eventually sold it.

Rodin's original model of this head was created for the lintel of his gigantic relief *The Gates of Hell*, commissioned in 1880. Rodin frequently readapted existing compositions, often endowing them with a new subject or context and executing them in different media. In this example, marks produced by various types of chisels are easy to discern. The rough character of the carving is typical of Rodin's preference for Michelangelo's technique, which left subsidiary elements of marble sculptures apparently unfinished.

Vincent van Gogh (Holland, 1853–1890, active in France)

The Postman Joseph Roulin, 1888

Brown ink over black chalk on paper

20$\frac{1}{4}$ x 16$\frac{5}{8}$ in. (51.4 x 42.2 cm)

The George Gard De Sylva Collection

M.49.17.1

THIS LARGE SHEET IS ONE OF THREE drawings and six paintings made by Vincent van Gogh in 1888 and 1889 of Joseph Roulin (1841–1903), a postal official in Arles and close companion of the artist. Van Gogh attempted to capture a sense of the character and personality of Roulin in addition to imparting a faithful interpretation of his external physical features. The postman's pride in his position is evidenced by the gold-trimmed uniform in which he poses and apparently wore day and night. Van Gogh called Roulin "a man more interesting than most" and came to love him dearly. It was Roulin, in fact, who brought the artist home after he cut off his ear.

In this extraordinary portrait, a replica (with some differences) of van Gogh's painting in the Museum of Fine Arts, Boston, the sitter's eyes are bright and his gaze even. Rendered in the artist's characteristic brown ink applied with reed pen, Roulin's snub-nosed face is drawn with light, rapid, vertical strokes, while the deep blue of his uniform is suggested by darker, more aggressively applied horizontal hatching. The portrait has an almost crude directness as well as an immediacy and poignancy that are hallmarks of van Gogh's highly personal style.

LATIN AMERICAN ART

Man-Jaguar

Mexico, Olmec, Gulf Coast, Tabasco, c. 1000–600 B.C.

Serpentine with traces of cinnabar

H. 4 1/4 in. (10.8 cm)

Gift of Constance McCormick Fearing

M.86.311.6

OLMEC CIVILIZATION FLOURISHED in the Gulf Coast region between 1200 and 400 B.C. and formed the philosophical, political, and artistic foundations of later Mesoamerican civilizations. Olmec sculpture, colossal in scale or exquisitely carved in jade and other precious greenstones, conveys a great monumentality. This diminutive figure powerfully portrays both the human and jaguarian features of a religious specialist or divine ruler undergoing transformation into a supernatural state. Transformation of humans into their animal companions was a means of engaging the ancestors and manipulating cosmic forces. The figure does not wear a mask but actually is, beneath his human form, a jaguar: the skin and hair on the head have been removed to expose his feline nature. The supernatural qualities of the sculpture were originally enhanced by glowing eyes inlaid with pyrite.

Jaguars have long inspired awe in the Americas and commonly symbolize the powers of kingship and authority. Though jaguars live in caves, they are equally at home on land and in water, and this ability to move between two realms led to their association with the act of transformation. Religious specialists and divine kings alike moved between earthly and supernatural worlds by means of meditation and the use of hallucinogens, and their actions were commemorated in effigy figures such as this one.

Standing Male Figure

Mexico, Maya, Campeche, Jaina, 600–800

Ceramic with white and blue pigment

H. 9⁷⁄₈ in. (25.1 cm)

Gift of Phil Berg

M.71.73.217

THIS HAND-MODELED FIGURE once formed part of a burial offering on the island of Jaina, located off the northwest coast of the Yucatán Peninsula. Graves on Jaina from the Late Classic period (600–900) usually contained one of these figures, which was placed on the chest or in the arms of the deceased.

While some Jaina figures appear to represent well-known deities, such as Ix Chel, the goddess of weaving, others may have reflected the occupations of the deceased, including warriors and ballplayers. Many figures also functioned as rattles, flutes, or whistles. Jaina figures were generally constructed as hollow or solid tubes of clay. The limbs and head were attached, the joints smoothed over, and the figure was then dressed with thin slabs of clay shaped as clothing. Pellets of clay were applied to create facial features and textile designs, then they were cut and shaped to fit the individual character.

This figure wears an embroidered hip cloth and turbanlike headdress. His raised right hand may have once held an object, while his left hand expresses the ancient Maya gesture of deference or respect. The figure's sloping forehead reveals his noble status. Traces of "Maya blue," a distinctive pigment central to the Maya palette, appear on his headdress.

Wall Relief

Guatemala/Mexico, Maya, Usumacinta Valley region,
possibly La Pasadita, 750–850

Limestone with remnants of red pigment

27 $\frac{1}{2}$ x 34 $\frac{1}{4}$ in. (69.9 x 87 cm)

Purchased with funds provided by Joan Palevsky and the Shinji Shumeikai Ancient Art Funds

AC1992.76.1

MONUMENTAL SCULPTURE OF THE CLASSIC PERIOD (250–900) portrays the kings and queens of the Maya and records their dynastic histories and courtly activities by means of an elaborate hieroglyphic writing system. This wall relief appears to be from La Pasadita, a hilltop site on the northern side of the Usumacinta River that was part of the political hierarchy of the dominant center of Yaxchilan.

Perhaps once situated in a royal palace, the relief depicts an elegantly dressed Maya noblewoman. She wears a long garment, or *huipil*, with embroidered edges. Her jewelry includes a jade bead necklace with a disk pectoral, wide beaded bracelets, and jade bead ear ornaments. The woman's headdress comprises the upper jaw of a serpent topped by a human mask and elegantly overlapping feathers of the quetzal bird. She sits cross-legged within a cartouche that represents the Mayan hieroglyph for the moon. The text panels indicate that one of her names or titles is the same

moon glyph. Partially eroded, the text records the woman as a deity impersonator, perhaps partaking in a ceremony. Bundles, such as the one she carries, often held effigies of the gods or ritual paraphernalia.

Labret in the Form of an Eagle Head

Mexico, Mixteca-Puebla, 1200–1500

Gold

$^3/_4$ x 1 $^1/_4$ in. (1.9 x 3.2 cm)

Gift of Constance McCormick Fearing

AC1992.134.29

THIS LABRET, OR LIP ORNAMENT, represents the fine artistry in gold work of the Late Postclassic period (1200–1500). Little of this work survives because the Spanish conquistadors melted down and cast into bars the many gold objects found in the treasury of the Aztec emperor Moctezuma.

Although gold working originated in the Andean region as early as 1200 B.C., metalworking did not appear in Mexico until the tenth century A.D. Smiths, who most often obtained gold by panning streams and riverbeds, frequently cast gold using the *cire-perdue* (lost-wax) method. They formed an exact beeswax model and encased it in a clay and powdered charcoal mold. The mold was heated and the wax melted out through a pouring channel. Molten metal was then poured into the mold to fill the cavity left by the wax. The mold itself was destroyed before the cast could be removed. For Aztecs and Mixtecs, the eagle not only symbolized the sun but also represented a military order dedicated to the sun. In the founding mythology of their capital, the Aztecs located Tenochtitlan on an island where an eagle perched on a cactus holds a serpent in its mouth, a symbol that endures today on the Mexican flag.

Mixteca-Puebla Style Vessel

Mexico, Nayarit, 1350–1500

Ceramic with pigment

H. 13³/₈ in. (34 cm)

Purchased with funds provided by Camilla Chandler Frost

M.2000.86

THIS VESSEL IS FROM THE AMAPA-PEÑITAS region of Nayarit in
northwestern Mexico. The complex, elaborately painted scene resembles
those found in codices of the Late Postclassic period (1200–1500). The
dense conglomerate of thirty figures wraps around the entire surface of the
vessel, including the bottom. A distinct scene involving six figures is
featured around the vessel's neck.

The Mixteca-Puebla style is not associated with a single ancient city
but rather with the many small city-states comprising a diverse array of
ethnic groups. Mixteca-Puebla art, generally small in scale, is found in wall
paintings and codices as well as in precious objects of turquoise mosaic,
gold, and featherwork. The Mixtecs of Oaxaca specialized in the painting of

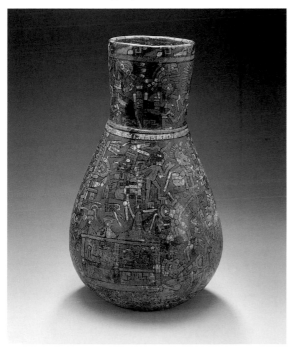

books and related forms of
painting on pottery. Some books
described the family histories of
the many dynasties throughout
the region. Others contained
religious accounts describing the
actions of the pantheon of gods
associated with the ritual calendar.
Reflecting the content and style of
these books, this vessel portrays
humans and supernatural figures
engaged in ritual and historic
action, perhaps associated with
the founding of a dynasty.

CERAMIC TRADITIONS OF ANCIENT WEST MEXICO

Around two thousand years ago, in the region now occupied by the modern West Mexican states of Nayarit, Jalisco, and Colima, powerful chieftains began building ceremonial centers. Their construction of elaborate subterranean shaft-and-chamber tombs was unique among ancient Mexican civilizations. The shaft-tomb

Kneeling Female Figure, Mexico, Nayarit, 200 B.C.–A.D. 300, ceramic with slip, 24 x 15 x 12 in. (61 x 38.1 x 30.5 cm), The Proctor Stafford Collection, museum purchase with funds provided by Mr. and Mrs. Allan C. Balch, M.86.296.1

Seated Male Figure, Mexico, Jalisco, 200 B.C.–A.D. 300, ceramic with burnished cream slip, 17 x 14 x 13 in. (43.2 x 35.6 x 33 cm), The Proctor Stafford Collection, museum purchase with funds provided by Mr. and Mrs. Allan C. Balch, M.86.296.85

cultures reached the height of their development between 200 B.C. and A.D. 500. The geographic distribution of tombs forms a rough arc through the lake and river basins of this mountainous volcanic region.

A variety of burial offerings were placed in these tombs, including large, hollow ceramic figures; models of buildings and festival scenes; vessels in the form of animals and plants; and smaller objects such as stone implements, shell trumpets, and obsidian mirrors. Figural sculptures commemorated various life events such as marriage and earlier rites of passage into adulthood. These occasions were marked by feasting, and the foods of the feast, both plant and animal, were also richly depicted in the art of West Mexico.

Scholars originally regarded the ceramic tomb sculptures as secular in meaning and anecdotal in content. More recently, however, the profound symbolic significance of the objects has become apparent through comparison with contemporary central Mexican polities, with which they were linked by trade.

LACMA's important collection of West Mexican ceramics was purchased from Proctor Stafford in 1986.

Standing Warrior, Mexico, Jalisco, El Arenal Brown style, 100 B.C.–A.D. 300, ceramic with red, yellow, white, and black slip, 37 x 15 in. (94 x 38.1 cm), The Proctor Stafford Collection, museum purchase with funds provided by Mr. and Mrs. Allan C. Balch, M.86.296.86

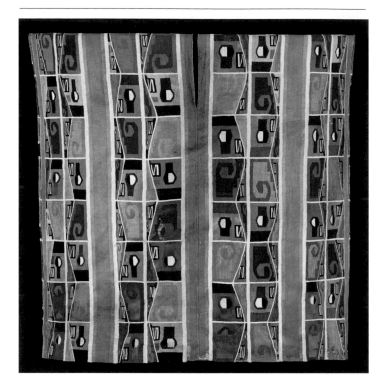

Man's Tunic

Peru, South Coast, Wari Culture, 600–850

Camelid fiber and cotton in tapestry weave

40 x 39 $\frac{1}{2}$ in. (101.6 x 100.3 cm)

Purchased with funds provided by Camilla Chandler Frost and Robert and Mary Looker through the 2000 Collectors Committee

M.2000.59

TEXTILES WERE THE MOST IMPORTANT commodity in the ancient Andean world. They played a part in tribute and taxation as well as religious and political ceremonies, including those pertaining to birth, marriage, and death. This region appears to have lacked a written language, but it is believed that much information was encoded in the design and imagery on woven or embroidered cloth. Many of these textiles survive today because they were wrapped in mummy bundles and buried, resting untouched for centuries in the dry, sandy tombs of Peru's coastal desert.

This tunic was worn by a male cleric or high government official of the Wari—people from the high Andes who created an empire that encompassed most of present-day Peru. Garments made in the labor-intensive tapestry weave demanded an extraordinary amount of material and human resources. The complexity of patterns, colors, and images suggests that Wari weavers were allowed wide latitude in their choice of designs.

The hallmark of Wari textile design is a focused abstraction of geometric motifs and stylized imagery that forms an iconographic "code," usually based on variations of a winged attendant figure holding a staff in profile. Incorporating a range of composite forms of humans, felines, raptor birds, and serpents, these complex abstractions may have symbolized the early Andean concept of a universe composed of complementary opposites and the interdependence among its human, animal, and supernatural spheres.

Chalice

Made in Mexico City, 1575–78
Silver gilt, rock crystal, boxwood, and feathers
H. 13 in. (33 cm)
William Randolph Hearst Collection
48.24.20

THIS CHALICE IS A FUSION of Spanish silver work and native Mexican craft tradition. It is conceived in the form of the massive architectural pieces of Spanish silver of the late Renaissance. The base of the bowl, the hexagonal knop, and the spreading lobed foot are densely chased in the conventional European manner with scenes and figures from the life of Christ. Instead of the traditional colored enamels, native featherwork has been employed as a background to the boxwood carvings in the hexagonal knop and the glazed compartments in the foot. Featherwork, a tradition that originated in pre-Hispanic times, continued into the colonial period and was put to new uses in religious art. The natural iridescence of the feathers greatly attracted the attention of Europeans and made the objects highly valued. The chalice also features rock crystal, a mineral that ancient Mexican artists had carved for centuries before the Europeans arrived in the New World in the fifteenth century.

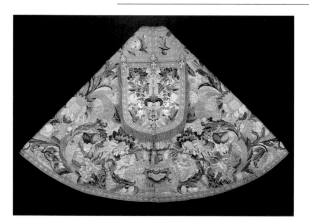

Cope from a Set of Vestments

Mexico, 1700–1750

Polychrome silk, metallic silver, and gold embroidery on linen

Cb. 53 x 112 1/2 in.

(134.6 x 285.8 cm)

Costume Council Fund

M.85.96.7

DURING THE CELEBRATION of the Catholic Mass, clergy members wear traditional ecclesiastical garments specific to ritual hierarchy and function. Originally based on Roman costume, the style of this ceremonial vestment was made into a uniform liturgical code of dress in the twelfth century that has remained consistent to the present day. Exquisitely embroidered sets of vestments lavishly worked with silver and gold were made in New Spain by nuns skilled in needlework or by embroiderers' guilds, which included members of the indigenous population who had been taught embroidery in schools run by priests. Nuns and professional embroiderers took commissions from Spanish and Creole (Spaniards born in New Spain) aristocrats for court clothing as well as for religious objects.

The exuberant color and pattern of this cope (a cloak worn by the priest as a processional garment) are characteristic of the eclecticism in the arts of Mexico during the eighteenth century. The indigenous style was influenced by new patterns from Europe and China, including the embroidered silks and tapestries brought by trade ships from the Philippines. The preference for intensely decorated surfaces and strong pattern had characterized native Mexican art well before the arrival of the Europeans, and a similar preference for the bold and elaborate was also evident in Spanish Baroque art. The confluence of characteristic motifs—brilliant peonies from Asia, pomegranates from Spain, and symbols of the sun and moon from Mexico—produced a richly colorful, stimulating amalgam of fascinating forms and patterns in the textiles of the period.

Carlos Mérida (Mexico, born Guatemala, 1891–1984)

Structural Study for a Mural, 1921

Oil on canvas

28³/₄ x 32³/₄ in. (73 x 83.2 cm)

The Bernard and Edith Lewin Collection of Mexican Art

A31997.LWN.323

ALTHOUGH CARLOS MÉRIDA was born in Guatemala, he spent most of his career in Mexico. Like many of his contemporaries, Mérida traveled to Paris, where he remained from 1912 to 1914. There he met a number of avant-garde artists, including Pablo Picasso and Amedeo Modigliani, and was in contact with Mexican artists such as Diego Rivera.

Upon his return to Guatemala in 1914, Mérida studied the country's art traditions and folklore, which he believed could serve as the basis of a higher art, one equal to that of Europe. In 1919 he moved to Mexico City, where he exhibited paintings of Indians composed in a deliberate flat style and in bright colors that recall Guatemalan textiles. *Structural Study for a Mural*, one of Mérida's earliest and most accomplished works, demonstrates his interest in representing subjects indigenous to the Americas. The swirling floral design in the background balances the strong geometric forms of the figures and echoes that of the handcrafted bowl in the foreground. These motifs reflect Mérida's interest in local folk traditions, which were undergoing a reevaluation in Mexico in the early 1920s.

Diego Rivera (Mexico, 1886–1957)
Flower Day, 1925
Oil on canvas
58 x 47 $\frac{1}{2}$ in. (147.3 x 120.7 cm)
Los Angeles County Fund
25.7.1

IN HIS VAST PUBLIC MURALS painted in Mexico and the United States from the early 1920s through the early 1950s, Diego Rivera created a new iconography that expounded socialist ideals and exalted the popular heritage of Mexican culture. He also produced a large body of easel paintings and graphic work. During his formative years in Spain and France from 1907 to 1921, Rivera experimented with Impressionist, Symbolist, and Cubist styles. Upon his 1921 return to Mexico City, where he launched his muralist career, he began intensively studying and collecting the country's Pre-Columbian and folk art.

Flower Day is Rivera's earliest depiction of a calla lily seller and one of his most important works representing the indigenous population of Mexico.

It is related in subject and style to his 1923 murals in the Court of Festivals at the Ministry of Public Education in Mexico City. The unusual perspective of the flowers, which are seen from above, and the blocklike forms of the figures are stylistic devices derived from Rivera's earlier Cubist paintings. The work's hieratic style also recalls Pre-Columbian sculptures. The success of *Flower Day* might have contributed to the ensuing popularity of the subject, of which Rivera created more than two dozen versions.

MEXICAN MODERNISM

Generally, Mexican modernism is associated with the muralists Diego Rivera, José Clemente Orozco, and David Alfaro Siqueiros, known as "Los Tres Grandes." They emerged at a time when the visual arts assumed an important political role in Mexico. After the Mexican Revolution (1910–20), art increasingly reflected a spirit of national pride and progress.

At the beginning of the twentieth century, many Mexican artists, Rivera and Siqueiros among them, traveled to Europe and

Diego Rivera (Mexico, 1886–1957),
Still Life with Bread and Fruit, 1917,
oil on canvas, 45³/₄ x 35 in. (116.2 x
88.9 cm), gift of Morton D. May, 53.25.1

became acquainted with the most avant-garde trends, including Cubism. Upon their return to Mexico, they sought to create a universal visual language that would also communicate a sense of national pride. They did so by drawing on stylistic elements that they considered Mexican and by selecting subjects that reflected the country's social reality. Folk art became a potent national symbol. Adolfo Best-Maugard and María Izquierdo, for example, based many of their compositions on the folk art traditions of Mexico, while Rivera portrayed indigenous types in many of his murals and easel paintings of the 1920s and later.

Although Rivera, Orozco, and Siqueiros are often seen as a group and are considered the prime representatives of the Mexican School, their approaches were radically different. Perhaps the most outspoken of Los Tres Grandes, Siqueiros was wary of equating Mexican art with the picturesque and the folkloric. He opted instead for experimenting with new techniques (he is credited with inventing the drip technique later adopted by

David Alfaro Siqueiros (Mexico, 1896–1974), *Landscape in Red*, 1969, acrylic on board, 26 x 40 in. (66 x 101.6 cm), The Bernard and Edith Lewin Collection of Mexican Art, AS1997.LWN.431

Jackson Pollock) and with introducing new ways of representing space.

During the 1920s and 1930s, a number of artists reacted against the propagandistic monumentality of the muralists and demonstrated greater affinities with other forms of vanguard visual expression. The Estridentista movement, for example, promoted the concept of an urban utopia not unlike that of the Italian Futurists. Los Contemporáneos disseminated the ideas of the European avant-garde and promoted artists such as Rufino Tamayo, who drew on Mexican culture but whose approach avoided the grandiloquence of the muralists. Many other artists, such as Frida Kahlo, who were not part of the Mexican School or affiliated with any group that countered it, contributed to the plural artistic discourses of Mexico. The influx of refugees from the Spanish Civil War and World War II further enriched the art scene in Mexico during the first half of the twentieth century.

In 1997 Bernard and Edith Lewin donated to LACMA a collection of more than two thousand works, mostly by Mexican masters.

Frida Kahlo (Mexico, 1907–1954), *Weeping Coconuts*, 1951, oil on canvas, $9^{1}/_{8}$ x 12 in. (23.2 x 30.5 cm), promised gift of Bernard and Edith Lewin, AS1997.LWN.615

Rufino Tamayo (Mexico, 1899–1991)

Messengers in the Wind, 1931

Oil on canvas

31 x 34 in. (78.7 x 86.4 cm)

The Bernard and Edith Lewin Collection of Mexican Art

AS1997.LWN.36

BORN IN OAXACA, RUFINO TAMAYO briefly attended the National School of Fine Arts in Mexico City and first traveled to New York in 1926. When he returned to Mexico in 1928, he grew increasingly interested in Mexican folk art and themes of everyday urban life. Folk art and Pre-Columbian art were important for Tamayo; he considered them to be true expressions of Mexican culture.

Unlike many Mexican contemporaries whose often politically charged work portrayed the native population in stereotypical ways, Tamayo advocated a universal art in which the act of painting would be valued over subject matter. He believed that art should have a primarily aesthetic rather than ideological function. Although the human figure is integral to his work, color and texture are equally significant.

In *Messengers in the Wind*, two native women dressed in white fly across an urban nocturnal sky. Their flight evokes works by the Italian Futurists; their speed is reinforced by the trajectory of the electrical wires. During the 1920s and 1930s, a number of artists in Mexico depicted the technology of the city to emphasize its modernity. This work conflates many of Tamayo's chief concerns—local subjects, urban life, and incongruous situations, which particularly reflects his interest in Surrealism.

Joaquín Torres-García (Uruguay, 1874–1949, active in Spain, France, and the United States)

Construction with White Line, 1938

Tempera on board

33 $\frac{1}{2}$ x 21 $\frac{1}{8}$ in. (85.1 x 53.7 cm)

Gift of the 2002 Collectors Committee and purchased with funds provided by Alice and Nahum Lainer

M.2002.55

BORN IN URUGUAY, JOAQUÍN TORRES-GARCÍA settled with his family in 1891 in Barcelona, where he became part of the Catalonian avant-garde. In 1926 he moved to Paris, befriended the Dutch artists Piet Mondrian and Theo van Doesberg, and quickly became associated with an international group of abstract artists.

By 1930 Torres-García began to formulate his own artistic theory, integrating symbols into his abstract compositions. He sought to create what he called a Universal Constructivist art, fusing pure abstraction with recognizable symbols that would prompt various associations. Like many contemporary European avant-garde artists, Torres-García became fascinated by so-called primitive art, and in 1929 he began incorporating patterns found on Pre-Columbian objects and images of ancient masks into his works.

Construction with White Line embodies the artist's desire to combine geometric abstraction with Indo-American motifs. Rendered in earth colors typical of Andean ceramics and textiles, the painting includes symbols recurrent in Torres-García's work: the universal man, the fish (a symbol of life), the pyramid (a symbol of reason), and the Pre-Columbian mask.

Matta [Roberto Sebastián
Matta Echaurren] (Chile,
1911–2002, active in
France, Mexico, and the
United States)
Untitled, 1940
Crayon, pencil, and collage
on paper
22 x 28 in. (55.9 x 71.1 cm)
Gift of Mrs. Lillian Alpers
AC1997.44.1

ROBERTO SEBASTIÁN MATTA ECHAURREN (known as Matta) is the
quintessential peripatetic artist. Born and raised in Chile, his career evolved
in Paris, New York, and Mexico, among many other places. He started out
in the early 1930s as an architect, working for two years with Le Corbusier
in Paris. By 1937 his association with the Surrealists (including Salvador
Dalí and André Breton) had led him to abandon architecture and devote
himself to painting. During his years in New York (1938–48), Matta served
as a bridge between American and European avant-garde artists and has
been credited with aiding the development of Abstract Expressionism.

Space is Matta's main subject. His work of the 1940s is characterized
by webs of lines that give his compositions an atmospheric depth. Known
as "inscapes" or "psychological morphologies," the seemingly ever-
changing forms are visual analogies for the artist's psyche. In this work, a
number of amorphous human bodies appear close to exploding into the
scene. Eroticism and danger are equated: The figures copulate and
dance—possibly a sly reference to Henri Matisse's *Joy of Life* (1905–6)—
and hold knives, which serve as both phallic symbols and tools of violence.
Although this kind of uncanny juxtaposition is characteristic of many
Surrealist works of the period, Matta's are unique in their conception of an
all-encompassing, intangible space, which is as much a representation of
the mind as it is of the cosmos.

Sebastião Salgado (Brazil, born 1944)

Untitled, 1988, printed 1990

Gelatin-silver print

16 x 20 in. (40.6 x 50.8 cm)

Ralph M. Parsons Fund

M.91.78.1

SEBASTIÃO SALGADO'S DEEP INTEREST in the human condition led him to begin studying law in 1963. Soon, however, he decided to switch careers and turned to economics; he received a doctorate in agricultural economy from the Sorbonne in 1971. By 1973 Salgado had changed careers once again, becoming a freelance photojournalist documenting the drought in the Sahel region of Africa. Later he joined several picture agencies, including the Paris-based Sygma in 1974, Gamma in 1975, and Magnum, the prestigious cooperative agency founded by Henri Cartier-Bresson, in 1978.

One of Salgado's most ambitious projects was his series on workers and the decline of manual labor as a result of the industrial age. The series was completed in 1992 and published as *Workers: An Archaeology of the*

Industrial Age (1993). The work comprises close to four hundred photographs taken all over the world, including Brazil, Cuba, China, India, Rwanda, and the United States. Among the strongest images are those taken in Serra Pelado in Brazil. This photograph shows numerous men climbing in and out of a gold mine carrying sacks both empty and full. The almost infinite trail of human bodies is dwarfed by the omnipotence of the landscape and contributes to the dramatic effect of the image.

Enrique Chagoya (United States, born Mexico, 1953)

Uprising of the Spirit, 1994

Acrylic and oil on paper

48 x 72 in. (121.9 x 182.9 cm)

Gift of Ann and Aaron Nisenson in Memory of Michael Nisenson

AC1995.183.9

BORN IN MEXICO, ENRIQUE CHAGOYA moved to the United States in 1977 and has since straddled both cultures. He brings together traditional icons from Mexico and the United States—Pre-Columbian deities, Disney characters, comic book heroes—to create images laden with new, provocative, and often political meanings.

Uprising of the Spirit is characteristic of Chagoya's interest in the dialogue and tensions between high and popular culture. Here, two cultural icons—Superman and Nezahualcoyotl, the Aztec king of Texcoco—are positioned for combat. Superman's weapon is his X-ray vision, while Nezahualcoyotl is armed with a traditional Aztec shield and club. Chagoya depicts Superman flying out of a scene derived from Theodore de Bry's illustrated book *America* (1590). De Bry's engravings documented the atrocities of the Spanish conquest. Thus Chagoya is equating American imperialism with Spain's massacre of the native population of the Americas. Nezahualcoyotl also emerges from an illustrated text, the famous sixteenth-century codex *Ixtlilxochitl*. A collector's stamp adds to the feeling of authenticity. Chagoya's battle is not exclusively among cultural icons or oppressors and the oppressed, but among the texts that construct history.

Cildo Meireles (Brazil, born 1948)

Webs of Freedom, 1976/98

Iron and glass

$59\,^1/_8$ x $59\,^1/_8$ in. (150.2 x 150.2 cm)

Purchased with funds provided by Cecilia Wong, Patricia Phelps de Cisneros, Carlos and Rosa de la Cruz, and the Modern and Contemporary Art Council

AC1999.13.1.1–8

CILDO MEIRELES'S WORK EXPLORES art-making systems and issues of perception and philosophy, and at the same time it reflects the political realities of contemporary Brazil. No piece exemplifies this remarkable mix better than *Webs of Freedom*. This work results from a systematic methodology: It is constructed from the repeated use of the same linear element. In theory, this work could not only extend indefinitely across a single plane, but it could also continue to grow volumetrically

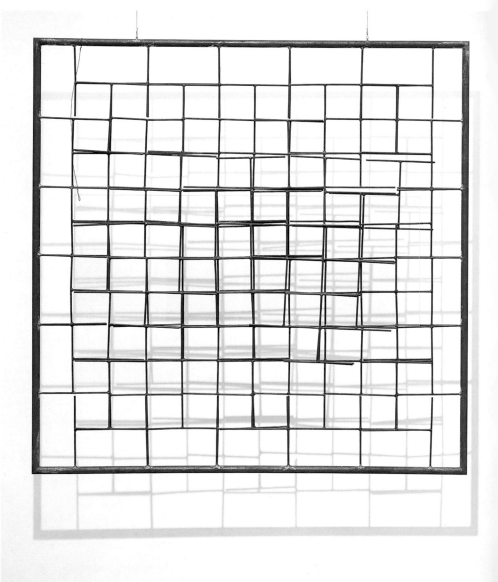

In 1976 Meireles made the first version of *Webs of Freedom* from fishing nets. In 1977 he fabricated it in metal. The museum's version (realized in 1998) is a foot larger in both dimensions than the 1977 piece and is constructed of tubular rather than flat iron. Separate elements (not shown in the illustration) that hang on the wall behind the metal grid represent its alphabet or building blocks. At first glance, the work seems ordered. However, the spiky angularity of the coarse iron grid, with a rectangular sheet of glass trapped within its structure, has more disturbing emotional and social connotations. The title is paradoxical, since webs suggest entrapment rather than liberty. *Webs of Freedom,* conceived at the height of Brazil's twenty-year dictatorship, is both an indictment of that regime and a statement about the nature of existence.

John Singleton Copley (United States, 1738–1815)

Portrait of a Lady, 1771

Oil on canvas

49 $^7/_8$ x 39 $^1/_2$ in. (126.7 x 100.3 cm)

Purchased with funds provided by the American Art Council, Anna Bing Arnold, F. Patrick Burns Bequest, Mr. and Mrs. William Preston Harrison Collection, David M. Koetser, the Art Museum Council, Jo Ann and Julian Ganz, Jr., The Ahmanson Foundation, Ray Stark, and other donors

85.2

JOHN SINGLETON COPLEY, THE LEADING portrait painter in the colonies in the decade before the Revolution, lavished his skill on the character and status of his sitters. The identity of the woman in this portrait is lost, but Copley gives us much information about her. Her relaxed posture and the quiet placement of her right hand over her left wrist are casual, but her eyes and face remain reserved and dignified. The dress she wears, while informal, is luxurious, and although the setting is private, for family and friends, even here she does not relax too much.

Copley was equally interested in describing the rich material surfaces that surrounded his subject. A rare piece of furniture in American homes of this period, the sofa, with its rich brocaded damask upholstery, competes for attention with the sitter. Americans might be plainspoken but they nonetheless liked displaying their wealth in expensive fabrics and highly polished furniture. Copley balances this extraordinary luxury with the quiet, almost severe expression on his sitter's face. She may live amid much comfort, but she is not taken in by it.

Armchair

Attributed to Thomas Affleck

(United States, born Scotland, 1740–1795)

Made in Philadelphia, 1765–75

Mahogany and white oak

$40\,^3/_4$ x $29\,^3/_4$ x $29\,^1/_2$ in. (103.5 x 75.6 x 74.9 cm)

Gift of Alice Braunfeld

M.2001.75.1

THIS CHAIR IS FROM A SET owned by John Penn, the last proprietary governor of Pennsylvania. It is attributed to Thomas Affleck, one of the best Philadelphia cabinetmakers and the only one known to have owned a copy of *The Gentleman and Cabinet-Maker's Director* (1754) by Thomas Chippendale, the greatest designer of English Rococo–style furniture.

The armchair was based on a "French Chair," plate 19 in the 1762 edition of the *Director*. The word *French* refers to the chair's straight legs, which were exceptional in the colonies in 1770, when most fashionable furniture had the *cabriole* (curved) legs that characterize American Chippendale furniture. The style of the chair, coupled with the outstanding quality of its carving and the ample expanse of upholstery (often the most expensive material in the household), demonstrates that it was intended to make a persuasive statement about the owner's wealth and social standing.

China Table

Attributed to Robert Harrold

Made in Portsmouth, New Hampshire, 1765–75

Mahogany, pine, and maple

$28\,^1/_4$ x $36\,^1/_2$ x $23\,^1/_8$ in. (71.8 x 92.7 x 58.7 cm)

Gift of Alice Braunfeld

M.2001.75.2

"CHINA" OR "SILVER" TABLES, as they were called in period accounts, were specifically designed for serving tea, a center of social activity in a wealthy eighteenth-century household. Such tables attested to the social standing of their owners, since their presence indicated a knowledge of the latest customs from England and the leisure time to practice them. Considered one of a family's most prized possessions, these tables were always fully set with silver and china and displayed in what was deemed the "best parlour."

Stylistically, this table is an unusual interpretation of the English Rococo (or Chippendale) in America. With its dramatically arched saltire (crossed) stretchers, the table is one of only seven known, all from Portsmouth, New Hampshire. It is characteristically English in style (only the use of maple as a secondary wood and the provenance of such tables reveal their American origin); its likely history is that an immigrant English cabinetmaker introduced the pattern to Portsmouth, thus demonstrating the cultural and stylistic orientation toward the mother country of the town's most affluent residents.

Tambour Desk

John Seymour (United States, 1738–1819) and
Thomas Seymour (United States, 1771–1848)
Made in Boston, 1794–1804
Mahogany with inlays of satinwood and pine
48 1/4 x 39 x 19 in. (122.6 x 99 x 48.3 cm)
Gift of Alice Braunfeld
M.2001.75.3

THIS DESK IS ONE OF THREE made by the leading Boston cabinetmakers John and Thomas Seymour to survive with its original pedimented top. The tambour doors, made from narrow strips of veneer glued to canvas, can be rolled back to reveal storage compartments. When closed, the delicate swags of bellflowers, painstakingly inlaid into each small strip, reflect the shapes of both the pediment and the drawer-front veneers.

Not surprisingly, since the Seymours had emigrated from London, the desk resembles a "Lady's Cabinet and Writing Table" illustrated in English design books of the late eighteenth century. It also reflects greater educational opportunities for women, since these lighter, more delicate forms were specifically developed for their use.

William Wetmore Story (United States, 1819–1895, active in Italy)
Cleopatra, modeled 1858, carved 1860
Marble
H. 55 in. (139.7 cm)
Gift of Mr. and Mrs. Henry M. Bateman
78.3

WILLIAM WETMORE STORY, an expatriate sculptor in the Anglo American colony in Rome, was assured his international reputation when this sculpture was sent by Pope Pius IX to the 1862 International Exposition in London. Like her historical counterpart, *Cleopatra* is both Greek and African. The sculpture gained its fame for its Neoclassical perfection and for its allusion to the fight for African American freedom. Story's best and most romantic works were large-scale seated figures of notable ancient heroines that focus on a psychological drama. In this early work, Cleopatra contemplates suicide after the loss of her Roman lover. Her despair and nervous tension are conveyed through a brooding facial expression, downcast head, slumped body, and agitated fingers. Nathaniel Hawthorne, who immortalized *Cleopatra* in *The Marble Faun* (1860), wrote: "He drew away the cloth. . . . The sitting figure of a woman was seen. . . .

Cleopatra—fierce, voluptuous, passionate, tender, wicked, terrible, and full of poisonous and rapturous enchantment—was kneaded into what, only a week or two before, had been a lump of wet clay."

Thomas Moran (United States, born England, 1837–1926)

Hot Springs of the Yellowstone, 1872

Oil on canvas

16 ¼ x 30 in. (41.3 x 76.2 cm)

Gift of Beverly and Herbert M. Gelfand

M.84.198

THOMAS MORAN, A PHILADELPHIA LANDSCAPE painter and illustrator, played a critical role in the formation of the first national park, Yellowstone. Moran visited the area with the earliest official government scientific survey in the summer of 1871. Working closely with photographer William H. Jackson, Moran studied Yellowstone's amazing landscapes and returned east to work his impressions into finished paintings. These efforts culminated in a monumental canvas, *The Grand Canyon of the Yellowstone*,

which was bought by Congress, as well as legislation saving Yellowstone from development.

In the same year, Moran painted a few other oils, including this view of the Mammoth Hot Springs, looking south toward Bunsen Peak. While *The Grand Canyon* celebrated Yellowstone's gigantic scale, this small painting was the first to focus on Yellowstone's most unusual feature, the hot springs. Moran was clearly impressed by the alchemy of mineralization that deposited a rainbow of colors in the stone. This work exhibits a hallmark of American landscape painting, the transformation of the wilderness experience into an emblematic work of art.

Winslow Homer (United States, 1836–1910)

The Cotton Pickers, 1876

Oil on canvas

24 x 38 ¹⁄₈ in. (61 x 96.8 cm)

WINSLOW HOMER WAS A SUBTLE CHRONICLER of African American life in the years immediately following the Civil War. During the 1870s he visited Virginia for a firsthand look at the work of Reconstruction, returning to scenes he had known as a war correspondent. The pictures that resulted from these trips analyzed the various successes, failures, and tragedies of the war and its aftermath. The most monumental of these studies is *The Cotton Pickers*.

The Cotton Pickers was painted in 1876, the nation's centennial year, when the state of the Union was much on the minds of Americans. During this period, Homer concentrated on representing his fellow Americans and their ways of life. Yet unlike most other commentators on American society, Homer included African Americans in this citizenry. These women are the first successful expression of the theme that would dominate Homer's figurative paintings in the last part of his career, the imagery of strong women who dominate the landscapes they toil in. The figures are seen from below, a perspective that raises them heroically above a sea of cotton. The almost infinite expanse of the field alludes to the enormity of their labor; their stoic beauty suggests the strength of their resistance to their condition.

Mary Cassatt (United States, 1844–1926, active in France)

Mother About to Wash Her Sleepy Child, 1880

Oil on canvas

$39\,^{1}/_{2}$ x $25\,^{7}/_{8}$ in. (100.3 x 65.7 cm)

Mrs. Fred Hathaway Bixby Bequest

M.62.8.14

MARY CASSATT WAS THE ONLY AMERICAN ARTIST to participate in the independent exhibitions organized by the Impressionists. *Mother About to Wash Her Sleepy Child* was shown in their sixth exhibition, the third to which Cassatt contributed. The painting is also the first of her depictions of mothers and children, the theme that became her most important contribution to the development of Impressionism, and one which constituted almost a third of her oeuvre.

Like the other Impressionists, Cassatt concentrated on painting contemporary life. Unlike her male counterparts, however, she was severely limited in the range of public subjects she could witness and portray. At the same time, as an early feminist artist, Cassatt upheld the special and positive character of women and women's domestic roles, turning a potential liability into a strength. In *Mother About to Wash Her Sleepy Child*, a mother reaches for a washcloth as she tenderly cradles the child on her lap; the child turns a sleep-flushed face up to her mother. The heart of the painting is the look that passes between them. Even though the subject is traditional, Cassatt's loose brushstroke and flat patterning transform it in a completely modern way.

John Singer Sargent (United States, born Italy, 1856–1925, active in England, France, and Italy)

Portrait of Mrs. Edward L. Davis and Her Son, Livingston Davis, 1890

Oil on canvas

86 1/8 x 48 1/4 in. (218.8 x 122.6 cm)

Frances and Armand Hammer Purchase Fund

M.69.18

ALTHOUGH JOHN SINGER SARGENT became the most successful portrait painter in the English-speaking world in his lifetime, he had a great deal of difficulty during the 1880s reconciling his desire to be stylistically up-to-date while still satisfying his sometimes conservative sitters and critics. This portrait was painted at the beginning of his American career, and it expresses perfectly the nature of his final triumph, his ability to stop just at the brink of being too daring, producing a painting that is both formally sophisticated as well as suitably flattering. This portrait was frequently exhibited and helped consolidate Sargent's fortunes.

Mrs. Edward Davis was the wife of the former mayor of Worcester, Massachusetts, and the portrait was painted at her home. Sargent posed Mrs. Davis on the threshold of her carriage house so that the background is cast entirely into darkness while she and her son are fully illuminated. The artist's technique and use of light allude to the Spanish seventeenth-century artist Diego Velázquez, as do the bolerolike jacket worn by Mrs. Davis and the sharp contrast between her black dress and her son's white summer costume. These allusions, however, are subsumed by the artful naturalness of the embrace of mother and son.

Winslow Homer (United States, 1836–1910)

After the Hunt, 1892

Watercolor, gouache, and graphite on paper

14 x 20 in. (35.6 x 50.8 cm)

Paul Rodman Mabury Collection

39.12.11

WINSLOW HOMER'S WATERCOLORS are remarkable for their expressive and inventive technique and for their dramatic subjects. In 1884 Homer permanently settled in Prout's Neck, Maine, but often spent late summer and early fall at a camp in the Adirondacks, New York, where he hunted and fished. *After the Hunt* shows the aftermath of a successful hunt. The deer has been driven into the water by hounds and drowned. Two guides haul a dog back into the boat; the body of the deer, already retrieved, lies behind them.

Homer depicted this subject from many different points of view and at many different moments in the drama. His deer-hunting watercolors represent his most sustained effort to record and imagine a single activity, and they are among his most important accomplishments. The subject is a brutal one, but Homer's astonishingly sophisticated technical control and simple composition force us to appreciate it as an aesthetic object. This paradox is the source of Homer's greatest power as an artist.

Henry Ossawa Tanner (United States, 1859–1937, active in France)
Daniel in the Lions' Den, 1907–18
Oil on paper mounted on canvas
41 1/8 x 49 7/8 in. (104.5 x 126.7 cm)
Mr. and Mrs. William Preston Harrison Collection
22.6.3

ACTIVE IN FRANCE AT THE TURN OF THE CENTURY, Henry Ossawa Tanner specialized in religious painting, and *Daniel in the Lions' Den* is one of his most admired works. According to the Old Testament story, Daniel, the Jewish prophet thrown into a lions' den by the Babylonian king Darius

for refusing to give up his faith (Dan. 6:16–24), remained calm, assured by his beliefs, and emerged from the den the next day unhurt. The theme of unjust persecution and imprisonment appealed to Tanner, whose mother and father, a bishop in the African Methodist Episcopal Church, were social and political activists.

The first version of this painting, shown at the Paris Salon of 1896, was more realistic, drawing on Tanner's academic training in Philadelphia and Paris as well as his visit to Palestine to study biblical culture. Reflecting his increasingly Symbolist approach, this version is less a literal narrative than an evocation of Daniel's experience, with Tanner conveying the prophet's tranquillity and spirituality through light and color. The blue-green palette with flecks of purple was a color scheme popular with Symbolist painters, who strove for quiet, meditative effects.

Writing Table from the Henry G. Marquand Residence, New York City

Designed by Louis Comfort Tiffany (United States, 1848–1933)

Made by Tiffany and Company, New York, c. 1885

Satinwood, brass, pewter, and original leather

$25\,^5/_8$ x 36 x $24\,^3/_8$ in. (65.1 x 91.4 x 61.9 cm)

Gift of the 1995 Collectors Committee

AC1995.46.1

IN 1881 HENRY GURDON MARQUAND, art patron and second president of the Metropolitan Museum of Art, commissioned Richard Morris Hunt to build a mansion at 68th Street and Madison Avenue in Manhattan. Marquand hired the period's most prominent designers to create the interior, which included a Moorish "smoking room" designed by John La Farge and Louis Comfort Tiffany. Moorish rooms were de rigueur in 1880s New York, but those that imitated ornament from the Alhambra (the fourteenth-century king's palace in Granada, Spain) exemplified the most elaborate phase of this style. The overmantel of the room was based on the Alhambra's Myrtle Court decoration, and the whole ensemble, filled with Hispano-Moresque lusterware and Islamic glass, was described in *The Decorator and Furnisher* (1888) as a "wondrously beautiful example *à la Alhambra*." This desk was designed as the smoking room's centerpiece, and Tiffany's fascination with Islamic architecture and design is evident in the desk's eight-sided shape, the molded arches of its base, the delicately carved spindled panels, and the arabesque inlays of various metals.

Quilt, Log Cabin Pattern, Pineapple Variation

Pennsylvania, 1870–80

Pieced wool and cotton

88 x 88 in. (223.5 x 223.5 cm)

Gift of the Betty Horton Collection

M.86.134.18

A PART OF AMERICAN CULTURE from the early years of settlement and western expansion, quilting was first a utilitarian act. As a cooperative task, it gave women in small communities a respite from their frequently solitary labors. Following an earlier period of reliance on European fabric and fashion, nineteenth-century American quiltmakers began to demonstrate a creative self-confidence paralleling the spirit of the times.

The Log Cabin square was an extremely versatile quilt-building unit. A center square of fabric was firmly sewn to a foundation block of cotton or muslin. Succeeding strips or "logs" of fabric were then sewn around it in an interlocking manner, setting up a lively visual counterpoint. In the octagonal blocks of the Pineapple variation, brightly colored angular pineapple shapes vibrate against a dark and intensely patterned ground, creating a dramatic sense of movement and depth. Other names of the Log Cabin's variant patterns reveal metaphors of their origins: Court House Steps, Barn Raising, Running Furrow, Streak of Lightning, and Windmill Blades. The museum's quilt is an enduring monument to the remarkable visual sense of the unknown artist who created it.

John Frederick Peto

(United States, 1854–1907)

HSP's Rack Picture, c. 1900

Oil on canvas

40 1/4 x 30 in. (102.2 x 76.2 cm)

Purchased with funds generously provided by Cecile Bartman

AC1998.140.1

A MASTER OF TROMPE L'OEIL (painting that "deceives the eye" through the illusionistic delineation of highly detailed narrative objects), still-life painter John Frederick Peto focused on inexpensive everyday things—envelopes, ledgers, newspaper clippings—their banality echoing his own modest lifestyle. Often he presented these items under strips of cloth, imitating the office "rack" (the predecessor of today's bulletin board). This, the largest of his "rack pictures," is dedicated to his daughter Helen Serrill Peto (HSP). His signature and her initials appear to be cut into the wooden backboard. Despite such illusionism and allusions to his life, Peto's late canvases reflect the artist's move away from realism toward modernism. Peto emphasized the composition's flatness through his choice of objects, then transformed these storytelling items into simple geometric forms (for example, he omits the addresses on envelopes so that they become simple colored rectangles). Design rather than allegory reigns supreme in his late rack paintings.

Table Lamp from the Susan Lawrence Dana House, Springfield, Illinois

Designed by Frank Lloyd Wright (United States, 1867–1959)

Made by Linden Glass Company, Chicago, 1903–4

Glass, bronze, and zinc

Base: 20 $\frac{1}{2}$ x 12 x 8 $\frac{7}{8}$ in. (52.1 x 30.5 x 22.5 cm);

shade: diam. 29 in. (73.7 cm)

Gift of Max Palevsky

M.2000.180.44a–b

THE PRAIRIE-STYLE BUILDINGS Frank Lloyd Wright completed in the first decade of the twentieth century redefined the concept of domestic space. Wright aimed for complete design unity—the total work of art created when building, furnishings, and setting form an environmental whole. Accordingly, the Dana commission included furniture, textiles, and light fixtures, as well as the house itself and its landscaping.

Wright called this philosophy *organic design*, insisting that a building must "associate with the ground and become natural to its prairie site." The overhanging eaves of the house are inspired by the low horizon of the prairie, as is the shade on the lamp—its pitch is similar to that of the house's roof. The Dana commission is linked by geometry and color as well as closeness to the earth. Wright considered geometric shapes the

"grammar" of architecture and design, which is acknowledged in the lamp by the zinc caning that holds the glass together. The glass, in earthy tones of amber, moss green, terracotta, and creamy white, mimics the colors of the prairie, which are echoed throughout the house

ARTS AND CRAFTS

The Arts and Crafts movement was more than an artistic style; it was a worldview that added design to the social reform agenda of the 1880s and 1890s. Its proponents believed that the industrial process had stripped the craftsperson of his or her individuality, and they vowed to change society by changing the very nature of work. They passionately believed that handmade objects produced from natural materials were morally superior to those made by machine, and that well-crafted objects had the power to improve the lives of the people who made them and those who used them.

Although the movement started in Great Britain, the most industrialized country in the world, it quickly spread to the United States. Max Palevsky's donation of more than three hundred objects enables LACMA to interpret the complex narrative of the American movement more comprehensively than with any other public collection. These objects demonstrate how Arts and Crafts

From left to right
Vase, designed by Frederick Hurten Rhead (England, 1880–1942, active United States), made by University City Pottery, University City, Missouri, 1911, earthenware, 17 1/4 x 5 1/8 in. (43.8 x 13 cm), gift of Max Palevsky, M.91.375.44

Vase, thrown by Joseph Fortune Meyer (France, 1848–1931, active United States), decorated by Mazie Teresa Ryan (United States, 1880–1946), made by Newcomb College Pottery, New Orleans, 1906, earthenware, 12 7/8 x 8 1/8 in. (32.7 x 20.6 cm), gift of Max Palevsky, M.91.375.31

Vase, made by Marblehead Pottery, Marblehead, Massachusetts, c. 1910–20, earthenware, 13 1/4 x 7 1/2 in. (33.7 x 19.1 cm), gift of Max Palevsky, M.91.375.27

practitioners favored solutions that had developed as a response to climate and geography. Made of local materials and reflecting vernacular traditions, architecture and furnishings were planned to fit into the landscape. The goal was design unity—a total work of art in which the building, its contents, and its setting formed an environmental whole. In furniture, straight lines replaced ornate curves, solid native woods took the place of imported veneers, and unnecessary decoration was rejected. The hope, never fully realized, was that these "simplifications" would reduce the cost of the products, making them accessible to a wide public.

The ceramics industry was one of the first to respond to the new demand for more individual, handmade objects. The illustrated pieces of art pottery share the movement's aesthetics and values: simplicity, inspiration from nature (rather than from styles of the past), integration of decoration and form, and individuality—all three were thrown on a wheel, and then hand

Living Room Armchair from the Robert R. Blacker House, Pasadena, California, designed by Henry Mather Greene (United States, 1870–1954) and Charles Sumner Greene (United States, 1868–1957), made by Peter Hall Manufacturing Company, Pasadena, 1907, mahogany, ebony, oak, and (replaced) upholstery, 33 $^3/_8$ x 24 $^1/_4$ x 21 $^5/_8$ in. (84.8 x 62.2 x 54.9 cm), gift of Max Palevsky, M.89.151.4

painted or incised. The chair from Greene and Greene's Blacker House exemplifies the Arts and Crafts movement's response to the local landscape (in this case Southern California), as well as the ideal of total integration, since the architects also designed all the furniture and lighting fixtures for the house.

George Bellows (United States, 1882–1925)

Cliff Dwellers, 1913

Oil on canvas

$40\frac{1}{8}$ x 42 in. (101.9 x 106.7 cm)

Los Angeles County Fund

16.4

GEORGE BELLOWS WAS A MEMBER of the Ash Can School, a group associated with the artist and teacher Robert Henri who painted the working-class slums of New York's Lower East Side, its "ash cans," as one critic said. *Cliff Dwellers* is Bellows's most complete urban street scene. Deftly conveying the storefronts and tenement stoops, Bellows focuses on the neighborhood's mothers and children, the domestic side of downtown life. The figures are almost caricatured by the few strokes Bellows has used to depict them, but the energy with which they are drawn holds the eye. Bellows made a related drawing under the title *Why Don't They Go to the Country for a Vacation?*, ironically calling attention not only to the poverty of the people but also to their humanity.

At the same time, a very complex formal order underlies the painting. Both the compositional structure and the color harmonies are self-consciously developed along the lines of the theorist Hardesty Maratta. This conceptual rigor, typical of Bellows and fully deployed here to manage the many figures and details in the composition, is one of the strengths of his painting.

Alfred Stieglitz (United States, 1864–1946)

Music Equivalent, 1922

Gelatin-silver print

7 x 9 ¹/₂ in. (17.8 x 24.1 cm)

Purchased with funds provided by Camilla Chandler Frost, Sheila and Wally Weisman, Robert F. Maguire III, the Grinstein Family, Alice and Nahum Lainer, and Dorothy and Paul Toeppen through the 1998 Collectors Committee, and the Ralph M. Parsons Fund

AC1998.126.1

ALFRED STIEGLITZ IS CUSTOMARILY REGARDED as the single most influential American photographer of the twentieth century. It may be said that his presence—as artist, publisher, and gallery director—not only assured photography of its modern position within the visual arts, but also went far in promoting modern art within the United States at the beginning of the century. By the early 1920s, Stieglitz felt that he had stretched the limits of his art, and he contemplated how the fundamentally materialistic vision of the camera could address abstract seeing. To that end, he began work on what many feel is his greatest contribution to photographic history—the Equivalents, a series of evocative images of clouds and sky. In an article published in 1923, Stieglitz outlined how he came to the subject: "I wanted to photograph clouds to find out what I had learned in forty years about photography. Through clouds to put down my philosophy of life—to show that my photographs were not due to subject matter—not to special trees, or faces, or interiors, to special privileges, clouds were there for everyone. . . . I wanted a series of photographs which when seen by Ernest Bloch [the composer] he would exclaim: 'Music! Music! Man, why that is music.'"

Music Equivalent of 1922 is from the initial set of ten images Stieglitz made that involved this radical notion. Later he photographed only cloud forms, with no indication of the landscapes below; here, he still situates the clouds above the earth, producing a spectacular visual poem to their majestic orchestration.

Anne Brigman (United States, 1869–1950)

The Soul of the Blasted Pine, 1908

Gelatin-silver print

7⁵⁄₈ x 9⁵⁄₈ in. (19.4 x 24.4 cm)

Ralph M. Parsons Fund

M.2001.8

ANNE BRIGMAN, an influential and idiosyncratic Pictorialist photographer working in Northern California, was championed by Alfred Stieglitz. Brigman became the only California member of Stieglitz's Photo-Secession in 1906 and of the British Linked Ring Society in 1909. Both groups were dedicated to furthering the understanding of photography as art. Her position as both a Pictorialist and as a member of the Stieglitz group is indicative of the times in which traditional ideas of the uses of photography as art and a rising modernist aesthetic were often at odds.

The dominant theme in the majority of her romantic and soft-focus imagery was the human figure in the landscape. Often posing nude within a meditative or expressive California landscape of weathered pines, precipitous cliffs, and limitless ocean, Brigman created images that reflect a bohemian lifestyle and a rising interest in transcendentalism. This use of tableaux and self-portraiture links her to Julia Margaret Cameron and her contemporary F. Holland Day. It also foreshadows the more conceptual pictorial investigations that arose toward the end of the twentieth century in work by artists such as Claude Cahun and Cindy Sherman.

Stanton Macdonald-Wright

(United States, 1890–1973)

Synchromy in Purple,

late 1918 or early 1919

Oil on canvas

36 x 28 in. (91.4 x 71.1 cm)

Los Angeles County Fund

60.51

THE PIONEERING MODERNIST
Stanton Macdonald-Wright
cofounded Synchromism with
Morgan Russell in Europe in
1913. Desiring to achieve
harmony and balance through the
systematic but abstract use of
color, the artist developed a color
scale not unlike a musical scale;
synchromy means "with color,"
just as *symphony* means "with music." With the outbreak of World War I,
Macdonald-Wright returned to the United States, first living in New York
City before settling in Southern California (the place of his childhood) in late
1918. In Los Angeles he was destined to spearhead the emerging
modernist movement of the region.

This seated, muscular male nude is constructed as a series of fractured
planes. Macdonald-Wright identified the dominant hue as purple, which in
his color scale was actually red-violet. The major color chord is the red-
violet, yellow-orange, and green that can be seen as a triad in the face. The
artist equated each color with a different emotion, and according to his
treatise on color, published in 1924, red-violet was "strong, rich in
potentialities." Historians have suggested that the theme of *Synchromy in
Purple* is creation. Painted soon after Macdonald-Wright's return home, it
signifies the artist's belief that California held the future for modern art.

Edward Weston (United States, 1886–1958)

Nude, 1925

Gelatin-silver print

6 1/4 x 8 1/2 in. (15.9 x 21.6 cm)

Anonymous gift

46.23.14

EDWARD WESTON BEGAN HIS CAREER as a photographer in Tropico (now Glendale), California. His work until the early 1920s showed a distinct Pictorialist sensibility that lent itself to romantic subjects, theatrical lighting,

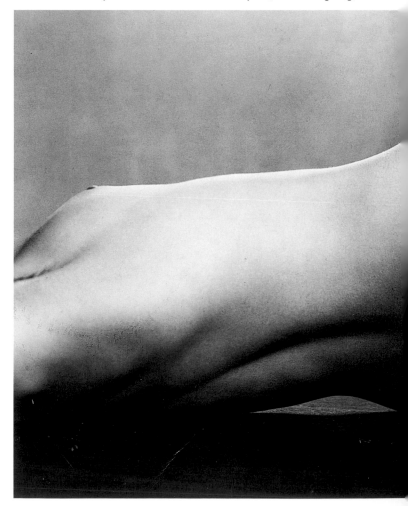

and painterly effects. Responding to a rising modernist aesthetic and a pivotal meeting with Alfred Stieglitz in 1922, Weston doggedly undertook the straightforward and unretouched photography of natural objects and scenes for which he became internationally known. For Weston, making photographs was not merely the creation of factual records or formally attractive compositions, but the communication of the essence of the object or scene before the camera, which he described as "the greater mystery of things revealed more clearly than the eyes see."

Weston's photographs of isolated and anthropomorphized peppers and shells; his lyric abstractions of rock, kelp, and tide pools along the Carmel coast; and his intricately balanced patterning captured in the undulations of the Oceano sand dunes are among his more renowned series. His intermittent nude studies extended his mastery of photography's potential to reveal through balance, precision, and a perceptive sensitivity the intricate abstraction inherent in natural forms.

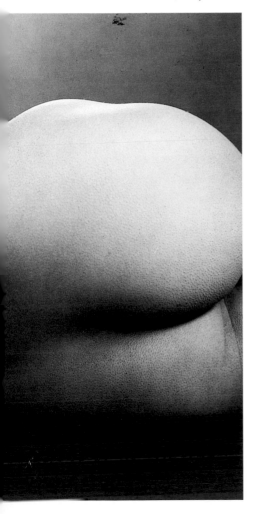

Imogen Cunningham

(United States, 1883–1976)

Aloe Bud, c. 1929

Gelatin-silver print

14 x 10 $^7/_8$ in. (35.6 x 27.6 cm)

Los Angeles County Fund

30.45.7

IMOGEN CUNNINGHAM first worked as an assistant to the studio and ethnographic photographer Edward Sheriff Curtis. After studying in Germany and starting her own studio in Seattle in 1910, she eventually moved to the San Francisco Bay area, where she became a dominant figure in the thriving photographic community that included Ansel Adams and Edward Weston. While Cunningham is perhaps best known for her beautiful and insightful portraiture, some of her most resonant images eschew the familiarity of faces and expression altogether. One of her early masterworks is this obliquely lighted and dramatically shadowed study of a lone aloe bud. Like other photographs of vegetables and flowers that she made about the same time, the image forefronts the bud's sensual form.

Aloe Bud is an early representative image of an important international movement in twentieth-century photography away from the romantic and painterly images of the Pictorialist aesthetic toward a more precise and straightforward celebration of the camera's potential. In 1932 Cunningham, along with several other California photographers—including Adams, Weston, Willard Van Dyke, and Consuelo Kanaga—formed Group f/64. Declaring their work to be "pure photography," they emphasized clean, crisp line and detail and exhibited a new freedom from painterly conventions for their aesthetic definition. Although the group held only one exhibition in 1935, their work had far-reaching effects, greatly influencing succeeding generations of photographers.

Georgia O'Keeffe (United States, 1887–1986)

Horse's Skull with Pink Rose, 1931

Oil on canvas

40 x 30 in. (101.6 x 76.2 cm)

Gift of the Georgia O'Keeffe Foundation

AC1994.159.1

GEORGIA O'KEEFFE WAS BASED on the East Coast until late in her career. While vacationing in the Southwest in 1929, however, she fell in love with the region, and after the death of her husband, Alfred Stieglitz, in 1946, she settled there permanently. O'Keeffe was fascinated by the desert ecology: the aridness of the land, the parched quality of its natural life, and the scorching sun. In 1931 she began combining found skulls and shank bones with artificial flowers and painting the simple arrangements as a "new way of trying to define [her] feeling about that country." These works received favorable attention when they were first exhibited in 1932 at

Stieglitz's gallery An American Place. From these early bone images she went on to develop her most iconic desert paintings, in which she set a single skull against a panoramic mountain-range backdrop.

Horse's Skull with Pink Rose is a transitional work. The inclusion of a rose and the use of a rich, dark shade of blue refer back to the large floral paintings O'Keeffe had created a few years earlier in hues of orange, red, and other vivid colors. This work retains the intense coloration of the flower paintings rather than the more restricted palette of earth tones characteristic of her later desert scenes. The skull, symbol of the desert, has been isolated from its normal environment in the same manner that the flowers had been removed from their garden. Only later when O'Keeffe returned the skull to its natural environment did she also utilize a palette of blacks, browns, and beiges that underscore the elemental character of the region.

CALIFORNIA ART: IMPRESSIONISM TO MODERNISM

For American Impressionist painters, California was a land wholly natural, drenched in light and joyfully colorful. They seldom approached grandeur in their paintings and instead preferred the comforts of the azure coast or the hush of the golden desert, as Southern Californians still do. The hectic pace of development around Los Angeles made every new arrival more acutely aware of the beauties of the land, preserved in canvases by Granville Redmond, William Wendt, and others.

Granville Redmond (United States, 1871–1935), *California Poppy Field*, c. 1926, oil on canvas, 40 1/4 x 60 1/4 in. (102.2 x 153 cm), gift of Raymond Griffith, 40.7

While local arts organizations were dominated by the Impressionists, the love of nature was not limited to them, and even at the height of their dominance, other visions thrived. Modernism still stands as the most convenient term for these styles and ideas, and Southern California quickly developed its own variety. Stanton Macdonald-Wright was the critical figure, encouraging an interest in different techniques and decorative effects. The influence of Diego Rivera and other Mexican muralists was also palpable. Realists like Millard Sheets reflected the dual interest in decorative elements and socially responsive art, capturing a California peopled by workers and the leisure class alike. Working in the Bay Area, Sargent Johnson in particular dedicated himself to depicting African American culture.

Millard Sheets (United States, 1907–1989), *Angel's Flight*, 1931, oil on canvas, 50 1/2 x 40 5/8 in. (128.3 x 102.6 cm), gift of Mrs. L. M. Maitland, 32.17

For such a small and tightly knit scene, the level of experimentation was surprisingly high and fluid. Connected to international movements, Californians were distant physically from Europe and New York but were unintimidated by that distance; they knew that they lived in the leading image factory in the world. Many of the artists were as

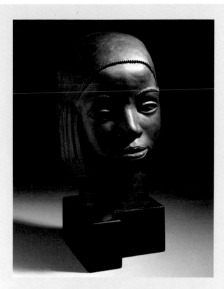

daring with materials and techniques as they were with imagery. Knud Merrild especially, with his assemblages and Flux paintings, was as vivid and innovative as any artist working in the United States in the 1930s. Without much support, but also without much opposition from well-established art institutions (for there were none), the younger artists of Southern California and their teachers practiced a wide variety of styles, laying the groundwork for the art scene that flourished in the region after the war.

Sargent Johnson (United States, 1887–1967), *Chester*, 1930, painted terracotta, 11 1/2 x 4 1/2 x 4 3/4 in. (29.2 x 11.4 x 12 cm), gift of Mrs. William J. Robertson in memory of her father Adolph Loewi, AC1997.71.1

Knud Merrild (Denmark, 1894–1954, active United States), *Provocative and Natural Form Organization*, 1933, oil on plaster and wood, 24 x 16 1/4 in. (61 x 41.2 cm), gift of Mrs. Knud Merrild, M.77.100.2

Lorser Feitelson (United States, 1898–1978), *Life Begins*, 1936, oil and collage on Masonite, 22 1/2 x 26 1/2 in. (57.2 x 67.3 cm), purchased with funds provided by Mrs. W. H. Russell by exchange, the Blanche and George Jones Fund, and the Modern and Contemporary Art Council, with the cooperation of the Lorser Feitelson and Helen Lundeberg Feitelson Arts Foundation and Tobey C. Moss Gallery, AC1996.103.1

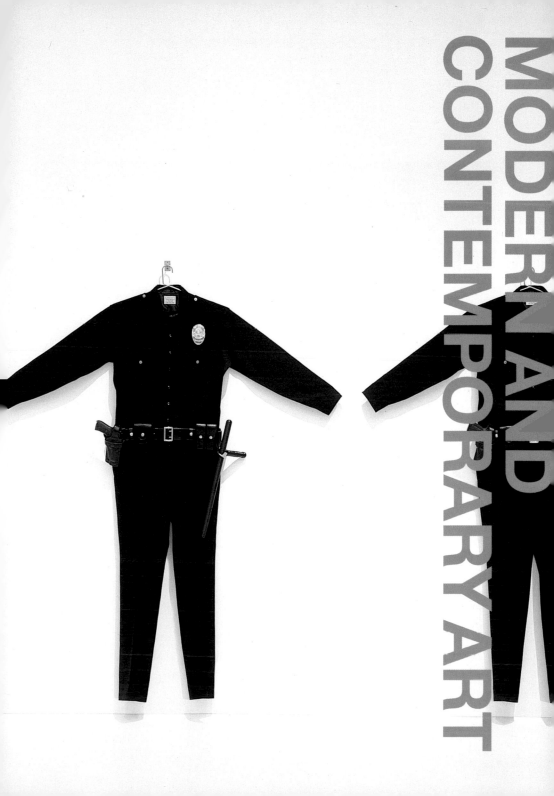

Mikhail Larionov (Russia, 1881–1964)

Dancing Soldiers, 1909–10

Oil on canvas

$34\,^5/_8$ x $40\,^3/_{16}$ in. (87.9 x 102.2 cm)

Purchased with funds provided by Mr. and Mrs. William Preston Harrison Collection, Mr. and Mrs. John C. Best, and Friends of the Museum, Charles Feldman, and Mr. and Mrs. Paul Kantor 80.3

MIKHAIL LARIONOV PLAYED A PIVOTAL ROLE in advancing the most revolutionary artistic thinking in Russia. He and his companion, the artist Natalia Goncharova, spearheaded what they termed a *Neoprimitive style*. They urged fellow Russian artists not simply to imitate Western European modernism but to find inspiration in unique, indigenous folk art practices. By including pictorial distortions and crudely lettered graffiti in *Dancing Soldiers*, Larionov borrowed from the Russian tradition of the peasant *lubok* (popular woodblock illustration).

Dancing Soldiers, based on Larionov's own experience of military service, portrays a raucous scene of soldiers at leisure. Two men engaged in a card game curse at each other, while a third drunkenly plays the accordion and sings a bawdy tune. By deliberately flattening the pictorial surface, Larionov makes the soldiers appear to float in an amorphous red space, heightening the scene's fanciful quality. The painting was shown in the 1910 exhibition in Moscow organized by the avant-garde Jack of Diamonds group, of which Larionov and Goncharova were founding members.

Natalia Goncharova (Russia, 1881–1962)

Ballet Costume for a Young Woman from "The Golden Cockerel," 1914

(1937 reconstruction by the artist of lost original)

Linen, cotton, and appliquéd braid

Headdress circumference 22 in. (55.9 cm); scarf cb. 22 in. (55.9 cm);

blouse cb. 18 1/4 in. (46.4 cm)

Purchased with funds provided by the Costume Council Fund

M.68.51.8a–d

THE BALLET *THE GOLDEN COCKEREL*, with music by Nicolai Rimsky-Korsakov, choreography by Michel Fokine, and costumes and sets by Natalia Goncharova, made its debut in Paris during the 1914 season of the Ballets Russes. The company's producer and charismatic director, Sergei

Diaghilev, initiated a dramatic change in the concept of ballet when he introduced the troupe in Paris in 1909. He saw ballet as a complete work of art—integrating music, choreography that expressed the emotion of the music, sets designed to elucidate the story, and costumes. The highly original and sometimes controversial ballets were a collaboration of the day's leading composers, dancers, painters, sculptors, and choreographers from Europe and Russia.

The Golden Cockerel tells the story of a half-bird/half-maiden who sets out to doom the tsar. Diaghilev wanted to blend exotic Oriental and Russian folk culture with the bold, graphic qualities of the new Russian art. He chose Goncharova because of her interest in Russian peasant folk tradition with its ties to eastern Asia, and because of her affiliation with the Russian avant-garde movement.

Based on the national peasant dress of

Russia, Goncharova's costumes comprised full, gathered skirts decorated with flat, bold patterns, simple blouses with brightly colored sleeves, and kerchiefs over cotton caps. The costume shows Goncharova's sophisticated mixing of traditional and contemporary art forms and prefigures an interest in costume and clothing design by other artists of the Russian avant-garde.

Marc Chagall (Russia, 1887–1985, active in France)
The Gamblers, 1919
Watercolor, tempera, and graphite on paper
15⅝ x 20 in. (39.7 x 50.8 cm)
Mr. and Mrs. William Preston Harrison Collection
39.9.6

THE GAMBLERS IS RELATED to a commission Marc Chagall received in 1919 to design scenery for a production of Nicolai Gogol's 1843 play of the same name at the Hermitage Theater in St. Petersburg. The influence of Russian folk art and mysticism that came to define the artist's work is perceptible in the drawing, which is characterized by bold and expressive colors and anatomical and spatial distortions. The spare palette of *The Gamblers*, as well as its simplicity and clarity of drawing and composition, bespeak its connection to a theater set.

The monumental and isolated figure in the drawing's foreground is Ikharev, the central character of Gogol's play. He throws his bilious green head back in despair, sickened by a universal corruption in which he is himself complicit. The absurdity and paradox that lay at the heart of Gogol's aesthetic held particular appeal for Chagall. A larger reading of *The Gamblers* suggests that it be viewed as a meditation on man's alienation and the capriciousness of fate.

Chagall had returned to Russia in 1914 after several years in Paris, where he observed and absorbed the lessons of Cubism among other early-twentieth-century artistic movements. In this second Russian period (which lasted until 1923, when he returned to Paris), Chagall was closely involved with the theater, first in Vitebsk, Belorussia, as the Bolshevik-appointed Commissar of Fine Arts, and later in Moscow and St. Petersburg.

Ernst Ludwig Kirchner (Germany, 1880–1938)
Two Women, 1911–12/22
Oil on canvas
59 x 47 in. (149.9 x 119.4 cm)
Gift of B. Gerald Cantor
60.33

THE YEAR 1911 was a milestone for the avant-garde German Expressionist group Die Brücke (The Bridge). That autumn, its three key artists—Ernst Ludwig Kirchner, Erich Heckel, and Karl Schmidt-Rottluff—moved to Berlin from Dresden, where they had worked since 1905. The pulsating vitality of this modern city was immediately reflected in their paintings and prints.

In *Two Women*, Kirchner depicted a pair of seamstresses on a Berlin street. The figure on the right resembles his friend Dodo (Doris) Grosse, who frequently modeled for the artist. Characteristic of Kirchner's work of this period, this painting is executed in strong colors and jagged lines, showing the awareness of Fauve as well as African and Oceanic art. He presents his two female subjects forcefully and directly and makes no attempt to beautify them; rather, he gives them lurid yellow complexions set off by rich black garments. This depiction remains less aggressive, however, than the many images Kirchner painted of hard-bitten and overtly sexualized young women on city streets, which reveal even more ambivalence toward modern urban life.

Kirchner resumed work on *Two Women* in the early 1920s in Davos, Switzerland, where he moved in 1918 following a war-induced nervous collapse. At this time, he heightened the contrast between various dark and light passages in the painting—for example, between the women's coats and the decorative cloth backdrop. On the reverse of *Two Women* is Kirchner's *Indian Dancer in Yellow Skirt* (1911), a seductive, barefoot dancer in exotic dress that reveals an interest in "primitive" or non-Western subjects that Kirchner shared with other Die Brücke artists.

Vasily Kandinsky (Russia, 1866–1944, active in Germany and France)

Untitled Improvisation III, 1914

Oil on cardboard

25⅝ x 19¾ in. (65 x 50.2 cm)

Museum acquisition by exchange from David E. Bright Bequest

M.85.151

VASILY KANDINSKY ASSURED HIS REPUTATION as a central figure in the development of modern art through his pioneering abstract work in Munich prior to World War I. In 1911 he and fellow artist Franz Marc formed the German Expressionist association Der Blaue Reiter (The Blue Rider).

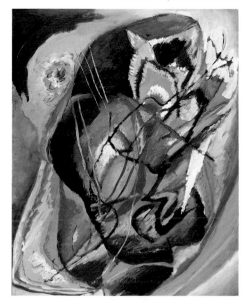

The following year, Kandinsky published *Concerning the Spiritual in Art*, a seminal text in the history of art.

From 1910 to 1914, Kandinsky painted a series of highly abstracted works called Impressions, Improvisations, and Compositions, terms he appropriated from music. These paintings are imbued with a turbulent, apocalyptic quality and contain veiled references to torrential floods, spear-wielding knights on horseback, and other evocative subjects. Kandinsky defined the Improvisations as paintings produced out of a sudden and unconscious inner impulse. The

Ludwig Meidner (Germany, 1884–1966), *Apocalyptic Landscape*, 1913, oil on canvas, 37 1/2 x 31 5/8 in. (95.3 x 80.3 cm), gift of Clifford Odets, 60.65.1b

Expressionism, an international movement in the visual arts as well as in literature, film, and theater, flourished in Germany between 1905 and 1925. The artists championed idealist values and sought to break free from the traditional restrictions of bourgeois society. They were principally concerned with expressing emotion and inner psychological truth.

The founding members of the pioneering German Expressionist group Die Brücke (The Bridge)—Ernst Ludwig Kirchner, Erich Heckel, Karl Schmidt-Rottluff, and Fritz Bleyl—created images of anxiety and the social alienation experienced in the growing metropolis prior to the outbreak of World War I. Their paintings, sculptures, and prints showed the influence of "primitive" art, with its simplified forms, deliberately crude figuration, and powerful, often jarring

juxtapositions of color. The members of the more stylistically diverse group Der Blaue Reiter (The Blue Rider), which was founded in 1911 by Vasily Kandinsky, Franz Marc, and Gabriele Münter, developed nonrepresentational images related to spiritual concepts.

For many Expressionist artists, World War I was a cataclysmic event that transformed their art. While the war brought disillusionment, further

Erich Heckel (Germany, 1883–1970), *Standing Child*, 1910, woodcut, 16 13/16 x 12 11/16 in. (42.7 x 32.2 cm), The Robert Gore Rifkind Center for German Expressionist Studies, M.82.288.370b

Hermann A. Scherer (Germany, 1893–1927), *Sleeping Woman with Boy*, 1926, painted wood, 19 1/2 x 13 5/16 x 21 1/2 in. (49.5 x 35.4 x 54.6 cm), gift of Anna Bing Arnold, M.84.30

Käthe Kollwitz (Germany, 1867–1945), *Self-Portrait*, 1934, charcoal on paper, 17 x 13 1/4 in. (43.2 x 33.7 cm), Los Angeles County Fund, 69.1

alienation, and death to many, it proved to be a core subject for the Expressionists. The subsequent revolution of 1918 provided an opportunity for the artists to join together in an idealistic effort to radically reshape modern society.

The museum has a particularly rich collection of German Expressionist art—paintings, sculptures, prints, drawings, and illustrated books. The collection was built through purchases and gifts beginning in 1946, when German-born William Valentiner became codirector of the Los Angeles County Museum of History, Science and Art (the precursor of LACMA). In the 1980s, LACMA established the Robert Gore Rifkind Center for German Expressionist Studies. This comprehensive collection includes approximately five thousand works on paper and a library of more than four thousand volumes, many containing original graphics, which were key to the accomplishments of the Expressionists. These holdings include not only superior impressions of woodcuts and lithographs by Kirchner, Heckel, Emil Nolde, and Kandinsky, but also rare periodicals and portfolios by Otto Dix, Käthe Kollwitz, and Max Pechstein, as well as numerous examples from lesser-known artists.

quivering brushstrokes, fluid lines, and saturated hues in *Untitled Improvisation III* combine to create the sort of work that Kandinsky believed would move the soul, like an inspiring piece of music. He fervently sought to reach viewers on a spiritual level and thereby combat the materialist forces that he felt imperiled modern society.

Untitled Improvisation III was formerly owned by the artist Gabriele Münter and then by Hans Hofmann, the Abstract Expressionist painter who brought the work with him when he emigrated from Germany to the United States in 1931.

Kurt Schwitters (Germany, 1887–1948)
Construction for Noble Ladies, 1919
Cardboard, wood, metal, and paint
40 $\frac{1}{2}$ x 33 in. (102.9 x 83.8 cm)
Purchased with funds provided by Mr. and Mrs. Norton Simon, the Junior Arts Council, Mr. and Mrs. Frederick R. Weisman, Mr. and Mrs. Taft Schreiber, Hans de Schulthess, Mr. and Mrs. Edwin Janss, and Mr. and Mrs. Gifford Phillips
M.62.22

THE YEARS IMMEDIATELY AFTER WORLD WAR I were filled with great ferment and experimentation. In this climate, poet, artist, and photographer Kurt Schwitters developed his own unique aesthetic, which he called "Merz." The concept was based on assemblage—the combining of ordinary objects with artistic elements. For Schwitters, Merz was an attempt to achieve freedom from all social, political, and cultural fetters.

Construction for Noble Ladies is one of Schwitters's large-scale reliefs known as *Merzbilder* (Merz pictures). It is revolutionary in its incorporation of everyday detritus—a funnel, broken wheels, a flattened metal toy train, and a ticket for shipping a bicycle by train—yet like the other *Merzbilder*, it remains an elegantly composed picture. A traditional portrait of a "noble lady" in profile, turned on her side and facing upward, is also included. These various found materials, seemingly whimsical and casual, are transformed into formal artistic elements by their arrangement according to Cubist principles. Embedded in the composition are hints of a narrative.

Georges Braque (France, 1882–1963)

Still Life with Violin, 1913

Oil on canvas

36 ¹/₂ x 26 in. (92.7 x 66 cm)

Purchased with funds provided by the Mr. and Mrs. George
Gard De Sylva Collection and the Copley Foundation
M.86.128

TOGETHER WITH PABLO PICASSO,
Georges Braque invented Cubism. Their
paintings from the years 1909 to 1914
seemed to grow one from the other,
indicating the close relationship between
the artists. Cubism was an art of everyday
life tied particularly to the cafés of Paris; the
works include vestiges of real-life referents
(wood-grain paper, newspapers, packages
of tobacco, and so forth).

Still Life with Violin is a transitional work between the two phases of
Cubism, the Analytic and the Synthetic. (The terms were coined by the
artists' zealous Parisian dealer, Daniel-Henry Kahnweiler.) Braque
incorporated the hallmarks of Analytic Cubism in his fragmentation of form
into multiple shifting planes and in his use of a restrained palette of browns
and grays. His depiction of wood grain signals the rise of Synthetic Cubism,
in which the fragmented planes are simplified, flattened out through a lack of
shading, and combined into often patterned forms that give the illusion of
recognizable objects. The wood-grained rectangle in Still Life with Violin
conjures up an image of a violin's gleaming wood surface; the S-scrolls
suggest sound holes; and the horizontal bars suggest a sheet of music.
Braque's use of the oval format, which he devised in 1909, is characteristic
of his Cubist works, as is his inclusion of snippets of floating typography
such as the one here reading "Duo pour" (duet for). For the Cubists, form
took primacy over subject matter.

Henri Matisse (France, 1869–1954)

Tea, 1919

Oil on canvas

55 1/4 x 83 1/4 in. (140.3 x 211.5 cm)

Bequest of David L. Loew in memory of his father, Marcus Loew

M.74.52.2

TEA IS THE LARGEST PAINTING executed by Henri Matisse in the years just after World War I. It marks a notable departure from the artist's Fauve work, in which he sought to transform his feelings into pure color. This garden scene depicts Matisse's model Henriette, his daughter Marguerite, and his dog Lili relaxing at the artist's residence in the Parisian suburb of Issy-les-Moulineaux. Although Matisse's use of sunlight evokes the Impressionists' attraction to painting directly from nature, he focused more on communicating the cool lushness of the scene through adherence to local color.

The masklike face of Marguerite, on the right, reflects the artist's long-standing interest in African art and contrasts sharply with the more conventionally rendered face of Henriette. In this sense, *Tea* is a logical

extension of Matisse's formative work *Heads of Jeannette* (1910–13), also in the museum's collection, in which he progressively abstracted the female visage in a sequence of five bronze sculptures.

In 1929 British art critic Roger Fry remarked that he found this painting to be "one of the most complete expressions of Matisse's highest powers." *Tea* was the last major Matisse painting acquired by Michael and Sarah Stein, brother and sister-in-law of Gertrude Stein and notable collectors in their own right.

László Moholy-Nagy (Hungary, 1895–1946, active in Germany and the United States)
Untitled, c. 1925
Gelatin-silver print
$9^{3}/_{8}$ x 7 in. (23.8 x 17.8 cm)
Ralph M. Parsons Fund
M.86.23

A WRITER, PAINTER, PHOTOGRAPHER, AND TEACHER, László Moholy-Nagy demonstrated a commanding talent in various arts, aesthetic theories, and art education. While still in Europe in the 1920s (he emigrated to the United States in 1937), Moholy sympathized with Dada and Constructivist artists who sought to erect a new aesthetic on the rubble of outworn bourgeois conventions. Moholy wanted to construct a new language of perceptions that would enable artists to take the greatest intellectual, spiritual, and aesthetic advantage of the world's emerging technologies.

In the 1920s and 1930s, images of the artist's hand proliferated as a Constructivist sign, symbolizing among other things the role of the artist's intellect and sense of touch in an ever-increasing mechanization of art. Moholy's image was a response to a montage made in 1924 by Russian architect and painter El Lissitzky in which an engineer's compass lies across the artist's extended fingers. Moholy's hand is a shadow, alluding to the mysterious presence of the artist rather than delineating the hand as one of many tools.

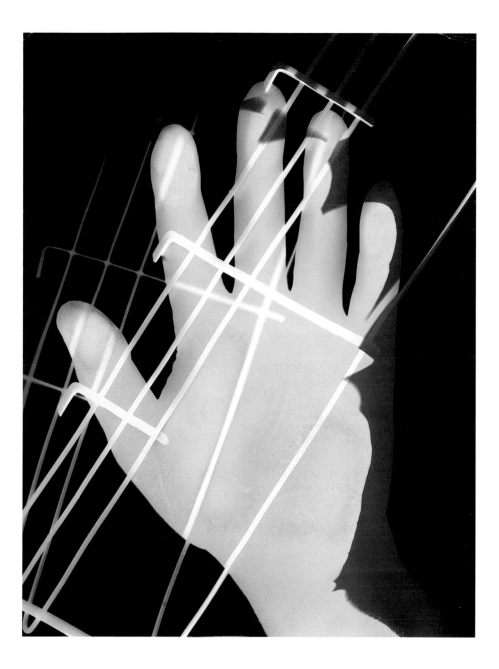

René Magritte (Belgium, 1898–1967)

La Trahison des images (Ceci n'est pas une pipe), c. 1928–29

Oil on canvas

25 ³/₈ x 37 in. (64.5 x 94 cm)

Purchased with funds provided by the Mr. and Mrs. William Preston Harrison Collection

78.7

LA TRAHISON DES IMAGES (Ceci n'est pas une pipe) (The Treachery of
images [This is not a pipe]) is one of René Magritte's Surrealist
masterpieces and an icon of modern art. Heavily influenced by Freudian
psychology, Surrealism represented a reaction against the "rationalism" that
some believed led Europe into the horrors of World War I. It attempted to
join the realm of dreams and fantasy to the everyday world.

Magritte's word-image paintings are treatises on the impossibility of
reconciling words, images, and objects. *La Trahison des images* challenges
the linguistic convention of identifying an image of something as the thing
itself. At first, Magritte's point appears simplistic, almost to the point of

provocation: A painting of a pipe is not the pipe itself. In fact, this work is highly paradoxical. Its realistic style and caption format recall advertising, a field in which Magritte had worked. Advertisements, however, elicit recognition without hesitation or equivocation; this painting causes the viewer to ponder its conflicting messages.

Magritte's use of text in his word-image paintings influenced a younger generation of conceptually oriented artists, including Jasper Johns, Roy Lichtenstein, Robert Rauschenberg, Edward Ruscha, and Andy Warhol.

Vasily Kandinsky (Russia, 1866–1944, active in Germany and France)
Semicircle, 1927
Watercolor and india ink on paper
19 x 12⅝ in. (48.3 x 32.1 cm)
Estate of David E. Bright
M.67.25.7

DURING THE 1920s, VASILY KANDINSKY was one of the most influential instructors at the Bauhaus, the experimental art school founded at Weimar, then later reestablished at Dessau. Previously in his native Russia during

and after World War I, while under the influence of Constructivists Kasimir Malevich and Vladimir Tatlin, the artist began to move away from the freewheeling and organic abstraction of the prewar years toward a purer geometric language. Kandinsky produced *Semicircle* during his Bauhaus period, when his predilection for geometric forms had fully asserted itself.

The circles, semicircles, triangles, rectangles, checkerboards, and squares that populate *Semicircle* are all arranged according to strict color and compositional harmonies carefully worked out by the artist. Floating in a sea of liquid orange, his forms defy the traditional relationship in painting between figure and ground. For Kandinsky the circle had symbolic and cosmic meaning: "The circle is the synthesis of the greatest oppositions," he wrote in 1929. "I love the circle today as I formerly loved the horse." Significantly, Kandinsky's drawings, which were often preliminary studies for paintings, achieved an independent status during this period, perhaps to a greater degree than before or after.

Pablo Picasso (Spain, 1881–1973)
Female Nude Kneeling before a Mirror, 1934
Ink, watercolor, and colored chalks on paper
$9\,^7/_8$ x $13\,^5/_8$ in.
(25.1 x 34.6 cm)
Mr. and Mrs. William Preston Harrison Collection
39.9.12

THE SUBJECT OF THE ARTIST AND HIS MODEL preoccupied Pablo Picasso at least from the late 1920s. *Female Nude Kneeling before a Mirror* dates from a period of intense graphic activity, during which Picasso was working on his famous series of one hundred etchings, the Vollard Suite, forty-six of which were devoted to the theme of the sculptor in his studio.

In these images, Picasso mingled the Neoclassicism that characterized much of his work of the 1920s with 1930s Surrealism. Elements of both styles are evident in *Female Nude Kneeling before a Mirror*, a drawing characterized by sensuous calligraphic lines and rich washes of color. The voluptuous modeling of the female form, with its cross-hatching and decorative patterning of tear-shaped pen strokes, gives the drawing a particular vibrancy.

The kneeling nude—her head thrown back, her arms raised, her mouth slightly open—seems autoerotically absorbed by her own reflection in the mirror. At the same time, a bearded man (a frequent surrogate for Picasso) peers at her voyeuristically through an open window. The act of observing, both passive (the mirror) and active (the model/muse, the voyeur, the artist, the external viewer), thus becomes the drawing's central theme. Its mystery and sexual tension are further enhanced by the candle, which provides the chamber's only light and casts a warm yellow glow across the model's naked form.

Pablo Picasso (Spain, 1881–1973)

Weeping Woman with Handkerchief, 1937

Oil on canvas

21 x 17 ¹/₂ in. (53.3 x 44.5 cm)

Gift of Mr. and Mrs. Thomas Mitchell

55.90

PABLO PICASSO'S LONG CAREER comprised several successive and radical shifts in formal concerns and, to a lesser degree, in subject matter. During and after his stylistic periods—Blue, Rose, Cubism, Neoclassicism, and Surrealism—Picasso explored themes in his own life and the world around him.

In 1937 Picasso executed his mammoth antiwar canvas *Guernica*, a protest to the carnage of the Spanish Civil War. After Picasso completed

Guernica he abandoned all but one of its motifs: the weeping woman. He drew her frequently, almost obsessively, for the next several months.

Tears all over her face, the figure in *Weeping Woman with Handkerchief* is an emblem of despair. Yet crowned with the traditional matronly mantilla, she is also the embodiment of Spanish womanhood. She represented Picasso's public and private agony: She was the victim of war, the grieving mother, the terrified peasant, the stunned survivor; but more specifically, she was a portrait of his lover, the artist-photographer Dora Maar, one in

PHOTOGRAPHIC SELF-PORTRAITURE

For some, the human face is a text that has to be read and deciphered. For others, there is no essential singularity to the face; it is always in motion, acting out, performing itself. Photographic portraits, whether traditional, modernist, or postmodernist, whether text or performance, can be construed as maps of the subject's inner workings. Self-portraits are even more revealing—charts of the most personal sort usually done in quiet complicity with the self. Even at their most distorted, fragmented, or affected, self-portraits have for the most part stayed remarkably true to their traditional values of unmasking the artist's ego.

Claude Cahun [Lucy Schwob] (France, 1894–1954), *I.O.U. (Self-Pride)*, 1929–30, gelatin-silver print, 6 x 4 1/8 in. (15.2 x 10.5 cm), The Audrey and Sydney Irmas Collection, AC1992.197.27

Solidified in 1992 by Audrey and Sydney Irmas's gift of nearly 150 works of self-picturing and added to periodically since then, the museum's collection of photographic self-portraits ranges in variety from Alphonse-Louis Poitevin as a solid bourgeoisie and Francis Frith dressed in a Levantine costume in the 1850s to Yasumasa Morimura as Vivien Leigh and Martin Kersels as a falling trampolinist in the 1990s.

Each self-portrait in the Audrey and Sydney Irmas Collection is a single image or a discrete set of images, a sample or samples of the self's reflection once removed. These samples affirm the artists' individual selves, not as shards or fragments of the psyche but as whatever can be imagined. Each self-portrait thus evidences the essential multiplicity of selves that were and are the artists', and in turn, by implication, shows that none of us is a singular self.

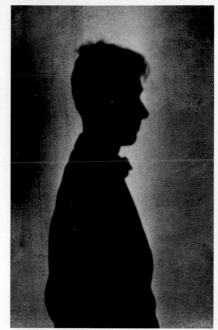

Walker Evans (United States, 1903–1975), *Silhouette Self-Portrait*, 1927, gelatin-silver print, 5 3/8 x 3 3/8 in. (13.7 x 8.6 cm), The Audrey and Sydney Irmas Collection, AC1992.197.49

Man Ray [Emmanuel Rudnitsky] (United States, 1890–1976, active in France), *Self-Portrait*, c. 1944, gelatin-silver print, 6 7/8 x 5 1/8 (17.5 x 13 cm), The Audrey and Sydney Irmas Collection, AC1992.197.86

Diane Arbus (United States, 1923–1971), *Self-Portrait in Mirror*, 1945, gelatin-silver print, 6 1/2 x 4 5/8 in. (16.5 x 11.7 cm), The Audrey and Sydney Irmas Collection, AC1992.197.4

a long line of Picasso's muses. Picasso's dramatic relationships with women informed the metaphors he used to express the intensity of his feelings over events in Spain.

Jackson Pollock (United States, 1912–1956)

Untitled, c. 1945

Crayon, pastel, and gouache on paper

$25^5/_8$ x $20^1/_2$ in. (65.1 x 52.1 cm)

Gift of Anna Bing Arnold and purchased with funds provided by Mr. William Inge, Dr. and Mrs. Kurt Wagner, Graphic Arts Council Fund, and Museum Acquisition Fund
M.87.65

UNTITLED EXEMPLIFIES JACKSON POLLOCK'S pivotal period from 1945 to 1946 when he shifted from the pictographic figurative references of his earlier work (heavily influenced by Native American art as well as Jungian psychology) to the gossamer fluidity of his mature drip paintings, the first of which date from 1947.

The thick black calligraphic lines, circles, and almond shapes of this drawing refer back to the figurative allusions and hieroglyphic notations of

the early 1940s, as does the masklike form hovering at the center behind a structuring grid of colored bars. At the same time, the loosely flowing curves of the black lines, interwoven with the straight, crisscrossing bars, look forward to the tangled skeins of paint Pollock would employ in the famous drip paintings. The effect of these two diverging elements—the delineating bars lying on the drawing's surface, and the more organic shapes and lines behind them—is to emphasize both flatness and depth simultaneously.

Pollock considered his drawings to be fully realized works rather than studies for his paintings. While *Untitled* is closely related to Pollock's oils of the same period, it stands on its own as a testament to the artist's ferocious creativity and independent spirit.

Willem de Kooning (United States, born Holland, 1904–1997)

Woman, c. 1952

Pastel, graphite, and charcoal on paper

14³⁄₈ x 12¹⁄₈ in. (36.5 x 30.8 cm)

Purchased with funds provided by the estate of David E. Bright, Paul Rosenberg and Co., and Lita A Hazen

M.75.7

WILLEM DE KOONING, one of the key figures of Abstract Expressionism, was trained in Rotterdam. He moved to New York City in 1927 and later to Long Island, where he remained for the rest of his life. Never succumbing fully to nonfigurative painting, de Kooning claimed that "even abstract shapes must have a likeness."

Figures of women dominate the artist's work from as early as the 1930s and can be said to be the central, crucial theme of his career. Particularly in the early 1950s, de Kooning was consumed with the subject, producing a series of paintings and drawings of enormous power and significance. The painting, *Woman I* (1950–52, Museum of Modern Art, New York), was the great, seminal work of this period.

De Kooning's pastel *Woman* belongs to the large group of drawings connected to the artist's Woman series (1950–55), and it may fall within a particularly impressive subgroup made in Southampton, Long Island, in the summer of 1952 that relates directly to the painting *Woman I*. The pastel also bears certain similarities (the yellow blouse and red skirt, for example) to another painting from the series, *Woman IV* (1952–53, Nelson-Atkins Museum of Art). *Woman* lacks the menacing presence of some of the works in the series, many of which have large, staring eyes and grotesque mouths with bared teeth. Instead, de Kooning has abstracted the figure's head to a boxlike form intersected by a swirling parabola that echoes the form's voluminous breasts, thus emphasizing the archetypal nature of the image.

Mark Rothko (United States, born Latvia, 1903–1970)

White Center, 1957

Oil on canvas

84 x 72 in. (213.4 x 182.9 cm)

The David E. Bright Bequest

M.67.25.21

ABSTRACT EXPRESSIONIST MARK ROTHKO is known for the hovering, shimmering fields of color in his mature paintings. In his early works of the 1930s, Rothko explored Social Realist themes, including works made under the auspices of the Works Progress Administration. By the early 1940s, he was exploring Surrealism as well as mythic and so-called primitive art. By the end of that decade, however, Rothko had rejected the representational subject matter of Surrealism and arrived at his mature style.

The color fields of *White Center* reflect Rothko's fascination with the emotional and visual power of the color red, which dominates his canvases of the 1950s and 1960s. The red rectangles suggest ritual and elemental associations (blood and fire, life and death), while an inner light seems to emanate from the white center, suggesting an ethereal, numinous glow. For Rothko, color was the key to a spiritual realm, evoking transcendental truths that could not be expressed through recognizable imagery.

Eames Storage Unit

Designed by Charles Eames (United States, 1907–1978) and Ray Eames (United States, 1912–1988), 1949–50

Made by Herman Miller Furniture Company, Zeeland, Michigan, 1951–55

Zinc-plated steel, birch-faced plywood, plastic-coated plywood, lacquered particle board, and rubber

69 x 47 x 16 in.

(175.3 x 119.4 x 40.6 cm)

Gift of Mr. Sid Avery and Mr. James Corcoran

M.86.105

PARTNERS IN LIFE AS WELL AS IN WORK, Charles and Ray Eames were polymath designers. From the 1940s to the 1970s, this husband-and-wife team created furniture, toys, buildings, films, exhibitions, and books. Working from their production studio in Venice, California, they expanded the borders of design, exploring applications of ergonomics and inventing new uses for materials. Important early advocates of new technologies and multimedia experiments, they believed good design in the service of progressive modernization could bring about social change.

The Eameses were guided by a fundamental principle: "recognizing the need." During the postwar era, they produced multifunctional, modern, well-designed furniture for the widest possible audience. Their residence, *Case Study House #8*, became a testing ground for their ideas about innovative, standardized production. This storage unit shares the same qualities as the façade of the house: a geometric steel grid with colorful panels. The first Eames cabinet pieces to be mass-produced, the storage units were designed as modules to accommodate a wide variety of residential and office functions. Compact, flexible, and inexpensive, the storage units were the perfect expression of the Eameses' aim to make low-cost, high-quality designs available to the average consumer. Ironically, the furniture was not commercially successful, and unlike their chairs, remained in production for only four years.

David Smith (United States, 1906–1965)

Cubi XXIII, 1964

Stainless steel

76 1/4 x 172 7/8 x 35 3/8 in. (193.7 x 439.1 x 89.9 cm)

Purchased with funds provided by the Modern and Contemporary Art Council

M.67.26

MORE THAN ANY OTHER ARTIST of his generation, David Smith brought American sculpture to international attention. He combined the teachings of European art history with American know-how. Smith derived formal structures from Cubism and Constructivism, added playfulness and symbolism from Surrealism, and found physical freedom in Expressionism. His blue-collar training as a steelworker brought a rugged and practical perspective to his work. The iron sculptures of Pablo Picasso and Julio González gave Smith the confidence and inspiration to use iron and steel, mediums he had previously associated with manual labor.

By the end of his career, Smith was exploring the medium itself as a theme: how steel interacts with sunlight, how negative space defines form, how lines in space may suggest human shapes. His final and most celebrated series, Cubi, is the mature realization of Smith's elegant and powerful geometry. *Cubi XXIII* is a study in light and mass; it does not so much occupy space as illuminate it.

In 1965 the museum was planning one of its earliest exhibitions, a show of Smith's sculpture, when the artist died in a car accident. The exhibition became a memorial to the man and his work.

Sigmar Polke

(Germany, born 1941)

The Fountain of Youth,

1984

Toned gelatin-silver print

50 x 110 in.

(127 x 279.4 cm)

Purchased with funds provided by
the Art Museum Council, 1992

AC1992.150.1

THE FOUNTAIN OF YOUTH is one of Polke's major works of the mid-1980s. It takes its title from a Renaissance painting by Lucas Cranach (1546, Gemäldegalerie, Staatliche Museen, Berlin), which is visible in the center of the photowork. Polke's photograph of *The Fountain of Youth* also captures the museum interior, showing two visitors examining the painting. Polke overlays an inverted scene of the exterior of the museum, visible only in an array of circular forms and a vertical strip along the right edge of the work. In this scene, revealed in fragments, a woman wearing a polka-dot blouse, a white glove, short boots, and a long, dark flared skirt dramatically kicks up her heels in front of the museum. By conflating these two views, Polke suggests that true youthful vitality may reside in the city's street life, rather than on the museum's walls.

Anselm Kiefer (Germany, born 1945)

The Book, 1985

Lead, steel, and tin

114 x 213 1/2 x 34 in. (289.6 x 542.3 x 86.4 cm)

Purchased with funds provided by the Modern and Contemporary Art Council and Louise and
Harold Held

M.85.376

ANSELM KIEFER IS ONE OF THE MOST ELOQUENT representatives of the generation of German artists born immediately after World War II who returned to the traditions of painting after the advent of Conceptual art in the late 1960s and early 1970s. Kiefer's symbols often have several layers of meaning. He also employs text to enrich and clarify his imagery, even creating books out of photographs enhanced by sand, metals, and straw.

The Book, a rare sculpture in Kiefer's work, is an iconic summation of many of his artistic concerns. It incorporates a monumental span of wings, a recurring symbol that refers to creative inspiration as a means to a new and better existence. But Kiefer's wings are also associated with Icarus of Greek mythology, who fell to his death when he dared to fly too close to the sun. Hence this complex object contains both the power of desire and the risk of failure.

The book itself is another of Kiefer's favored symbols, connoting knowledge that can result in both good and evil. The specter of history, particularly the history of German nationalism, haunts Kiefer's work, and his awareness of Jews as the people of the Book adds further meaning to the sculpture. The lead surface of *The Book* is metaphorically significant; heavy and antithetical to flight, this metal was also used by medieval alchemists who attempted to turn base elements into gold. Every aspect of this work, including its great size, conveys Kiefer's intense aspirations.

Edward Kienholz (United States, 1927–1994), *Back Seat Dodge '38*, 1964, mixed media, 66 x 240 x 144 in. (167.6 x 609.6 x 365.8 cm), purchased with funds provided by the Art Museum Council, M.81.248a–e

With thousands of objects by California artists amassed by six curatorial departments, the museum's collections reflect the historical development of art in California from the early years of the twentieth century to the region's ascendance as an international center for the creation of contemporary art.

Especially well represented is art made since 1965, when the museum was established as an independent institution. In the 1960s, Los Angeles–based artist Craig Kauffman was one of a group of artists who used vacuum-formed plastics, vapor-coated glass, and luminous pigments to impart an ethereal quality to his work. Other artists used less sleek materials. Edward Kienholz's evocative tableaux—*Back Seat Dodge '38*, for example—used found objects, such as a junked automobile, to create assemblages that were laden with political, psychological, or spiritual meanings. Edward Ruscha and Eleanor Antin explored language- and narrative-based forms and were among the pioneers of Pop and Conceptual art. Recent California art at the museum ranges from landscape photography evoking the sublime by Sharon Lockhart to Chris Burden's oversize police uniforms that reflect contemporary social anxieties.

Fine art printmaking by Southern California workshops is also represented at the museum. From the 1960s, the Tamarind Lithography Workshop, Gemini G.E.L., and Cirrus

Edward Ruscha (United States, born 1937), *Actual Size*, 1962, oil on canvas, 72 x 67 in. (182.9 x 170.2 cm), anonymous gift through the Contemporary Art Council, M.63.14

Chris Burden (United States, born 1931), *L.A.P.D. Uniforms*, 1993, fabric, leather, wood, metal, and plastic, 88 x 72 x 6 in. (223.5 x 182.9 x 15.2 cm) each, purchased with funds provided by the Modern and Contemporary Art Council, M.2000.151.1–4

Bruce Nauman (United States, born 1941), *Raw-War*, 1971, 3-color lithograph on Arches paper, printed in 3 runs from 3 matrices (stones and aluminum plates), 22 1/2 x 28 1/4 in. (57.2 x 71.8 cm), Cirrus Editions Archive, purchased with funds provided by the Director's Roundtable, and gift of Cirrus Editions, M.86.2.678

Editions have dramatically fostered the cosmopolitanism of the Los Angeles art scene. Begun in the 1970s, Self-Help Graphics supported the Chicano political and cultural movement. In addition to publishing such major California artists as Vija Celmins and Bruce Nauman, these four workshops attracted hundreds of international figures, including Rufino Tamayo, Robert Rauschenberg, and Roy Lichtenstein, who spent time in Los Angeles.

Southern California has also been a leader in setting fashion trends. Beginning in the 1930s, a number of prominent Hollywood movie costume designers—including Adrian, Irene, Bonnie Cashin, Howard Greer, and Jean-Louis—extended successful careers by opening their own couture houses, and some of their signature work forms the museum's in-depth collections. Southern California's beach culture influenced the development of American swimwear, while the region's year-round indoor/outdoor lifestyle gave rise to the casually stylish American sportswear ensemble. Rudi Gernreich's visionary designs, which influenced pop culture during the turbulent 1960s, and the elegant haute couture of James Galanos are extensively represented in the museum's collections.

Rudi Gernreich (Austria, 1922–1985, active in the United States), *Tunic and Pants*, 1968, wool knit with metal hooks and leather trim, cb. 30 in. (76.2 cm), inseam 31 in. (78.7 cm), gift of Tomi Kuwayama, AC1999.205.1.1–2

David Hockney (England, born 1937, active in the United States)

Mulholland Drive: The Road to the Studio, 1980

Acrylic on canvas

86 x 243 in. (218.4 x 617.2 cm)

Purchased with funds provided by the F. Patrick Burns Bequest

M.83.35

AFTER A BRILLIANT CAREER at the Royal College of Art in London and having already achieved international fame as a Pop artist, the young and multitalented David Hockney left his native England for Los Angeles in the early 1960s. "Within a week of arriving there in this strange big city, not knowing a soul, I'd passed the driving test, bought a car, driven to Las Vegas and won some money, got myself a studio, started painting, all within a week. And I thought, it's just how I imagined it would be." Perhaps it is his outsider's perspective that gives Hockney such fondness for his adopted hometown; his long and varied career in painting, photography, writing, stage design, and other endeavors has frequently paid homage to the distinctive atmosphere that pervades Los Angeles. Hockney revels in the sea, sun, sky, canyons, handsome young men, and overindulgent luxuries that have come to characterize Southern California.

Mulholland Drive: The Road to the Studio, Hockney's largest single canvas, is based on his experience of daily drives along the curving hillcrest road to and from his studio; it reads from left to right following the artist's

journey across the landscape. The San Fernando Valley in the background is depicted in maplike lines. Certain details—grass and foliage—are carefully rendered and stand out vividly while others are generalized, as if blurred in Hockney's peripheral vision. Hockney uses bright, daring color, explaining, "I like it and surround myself with it because I think, frankly, it makes life a bit more joyful."

Sherrie Levine (United States, born 1947)

Crystal Newborn, 1993; *Black Newborn*, 1994

Cast and sandblasted glass

5 x 8 x 8¹⁄₂ in. (12.7 x 20.3 x 21.6 cm) each

Gift of Daniel Greenberg and Susan Steinhauser;
Purchased with funds provided by
Daniel Greenberg and Susan Steinhauser
AC1997.249.31; AC1995.87.1

SHERRIE LEVINE CREATED TWO EDITIONS (each of twelve) of *Newborn*, one in translucent, frosted white glass and the other in black glass. Both versions were cast from Constantin Brancusi's 1915 marble sculpture of the same name in the collection of the Philadelphia Museum of Art.

In the creation of these elegant objects, Levine utilized the notion of appropriation that she helped to define in the early 1980s. By brazenly toying with the idea of plagiarism, Levine calls attention to the conventional recycling of aesthetic forms, thus questioning whether any art is truly

original. Her various copying techniques—rephotography, redrawing, and, in this case, casting from another medium—undercut the concept of uniqueness that has been essential to the historical and commercial appraisal of the "authentic" art object.

Ambivalence is central to Levine's project. Although she seeks to undermine the celebration of individual "genius" that has dominated many histories of modernism, she also has great affection for the art she usurps. While her appropriations criticize, they also express a longing for the heroism of high modernism at a time when one of its most defining characteristics, newness, no longer seems attainable. The irony is that by adopting Brancusi's sculpture as a means of acknowledging this dilemma, Levine has reincarnated that work into something novel. Under her aegis the title *Newborn* becomes a purposeful double entendre.

Bill Viola (United States, born 1951)
Slowly Turning Narrative, 1992
Video-sound installation with rotating screen
14 x 20 x 490 ft. (4.3 x 6.1 x 12.5 m)
Purchased with funds provided by the Modern and Contemporary Art Council
AC1995.146.1

BILL VIOLA, A MEMBER OF THE FIRST GENERATION to grow up with television, is an acclaimed pioneer of the medium of video art. Encountering his *Slowly Turning Narrative*, the viewer enters a darkened gallery where overhead projectors are aimed from opposite sides of the room onto a rotating plane perpendicular to the floor in the center. One surface of the plane is a white screen that receives the video projections, while the obverse surface is a mirror that casts the reflected images around the walls of the room.

One projection features a colorful procession of vignettes of daily human activity and life: newborn babies, children at play, people at work, automobile accidents, lovers, celebrations, city life, nature—a catalogue of everything that constitutes the world we inhabit and the events that construct our individual histories. The other is a black-and-white projection of a close-up of the artist reciting the phrases "the one who knows," "the one who cries," "the one who reads," "the one who loves," "the one who believes," and so on. His incantation evokes human consciousness and the reflective nature of humankind. The reeling images at the center of the room and coursing its perimeter thus enfold the viewer in a colloquy between the daily events of the physical world and the contemplative self, which has the uniquely human capacity to reflect on and ascribe meaning to life.

PHOTOGRAPHY CREDITS

Most photographs are reproduced courtesy of the creators and lenders of the material depicted. For certain artwork and documentary photographs we have been unable to trace copyright holders. We would appreciate notification of additional credits for acknowledgment in future editions.

INDEX OF ARTISTS